About the Author

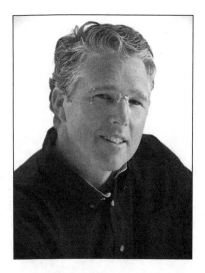

Brady G. Wilson is the co-founder of Juice Inc., a solution provider for leaders who want to boost their organizational energy levels and employee engagement. He has unleashed profitable results for leaders, managers, and sales professionals in many of North America's Fortune 500 companies. His passion for creating breakthroughs for companies has spawned such innovative tools and programs as Pull Conversations™, The Five Drivers of Engagement™, and The Juice Check™. He lives in Guelph, Ontario.

RELEASE
YOUR COMPANY'S
Intelligent Energy
THROUGH POWERFUL
CONVERSATIONS

BRADY G. WILSON

FOREWORD BY JOHN WRIGHT

BASTIAN
BOOKS

Bastian Books
Toronto, Canada
A division of Bastian Publishing Services Ltd.
www.bastianpubserv.com

Distributed by Publishers Group Canada
www.pgcbooks.ca

ISBN 0-9780554-1-1

Cataloguing in Publication Data available from
Library and Archives Canada

Note: Great care has been taken care to protect the identities of the people in the following stories. Where individuals' real names have been used, as indicated in brackets, we have received permission to do so. Every effort has been made to identify, obtain permission from, and credit all sources. The publisher would appreciate notification of omissions or errors so that they may be corrected. Chapter 1 excerpt from *Communication World*, July–August 2004, courtesy of International Association of Business Communicators. Chapter 4 excerpt from *The Language of Love* excerpted and adapted from *The Language of Love* by Gary Smalley and John Trent, Ph.D., a Focus on the Family book published by Tyndale House Publishers. Copyright © 1988, 1991, 2006 by Gary Smalley and John Trent, Ph.D. All rights reserved. International copyright secured. Used by permission. Chapter 6 excerpt from "Tell Me More: On the Art of Listening" by Brenda Ueland from *Strength to Your Sword Arm: Selected Writings by Brenda Ueland* (Holy Cow! Press, 1993). Used by permission of the Estate of Brenda Ueland and Holy Cow! Press. All rights reserved.

Editorial: Donald G. Bastian, Bastian Publishing Services Ltd.
www.bastianpubserv.com

Cover and interior design: Daniel Crack, Kinetics Design

Printed and bound in Canada by Webcom
Reprinted February 2007

To the memory of J.C. Wilson,
my Dad,
a man who pulled more laughter out of life
than anyone I have ever known

Contents

Foreword

*A*FTER working for twenty-five years in the communications and public affairs arena, and after spending the last seventeen years looking at absolutely every dimension of public opinion imaginable, both out of curiosity and on behalf of many clients, I have learned one truth that transcends all other truths I've ever learned, and that is this: It's the simplest things that are the most profound and the most likely to make a difference in whatever we're trying to accomplish.

Brady Wilson and his business partner, Alex Somos, have found, and implemented, some simple and central truths about the workplace. That was clear to me when I first met them and it's even clearer to me today, now that I have read this book.

I was very excited, a few years back, when they asked me to do some public opinion research among employees in the workplace. For lack of a better metaphor, I was "juiced" by their assignment. I instantly grasped, from their spirit and their questions, the simplicity and profundity of their approach to work and life.

In my world you can ask 100 questions and then sit and look at data tables at least 300 pages thick and be no further ahead then when you started. Unless, that is, you know three things: the story in the data, be it of romance and adventure, or challenge and inspiration, or anything else; the context, without which the data will not make sense; and concrete examples that anchor and illustrate the findings.

Brady and Alex provided me with these three essentials. They showed me that in a world of bits and bytes of information, zipping and zapping around from emails and videoconferences and pod-casts and Web streaming, the most important element in the workplace and beyond had been lost: conversations between human beings.

And when we stop to think about it, we all know that the empathy of human relationships and the ability to motivate people have been sucked out of almost every dimension of the workplace as technology has made it easier and faster for us to communicate our thoughts and information.

Anyone who works in the workplace today can relate to this. Managers and people involved with clients in service relations can, if they choose, hide behind their computer screens, and elude the office with their BlackBerries, almost all day (and night). They can communicate without ever being heard or met – or understood. Ours has become a push-key world in which commands and ideas are pushed out and onto people, with the human touch so diminished that workers and others argue over whether or not email phrasing can have a personal tone.

The following pages are profound and incredibly energizing because they say to managers and workers alike that engaging with others in a very simple, contextual, and *human* way in the workplace can produce extraordinary results. This book is backed up with numerous examples and written so that once you start reading it you won't put it down until you're done. Through it, Brady Wilson provides the way to navigate, nurture, and necessitate the most productive relationships possible.

If the Tom Peters maxim of "managing by wandering around"

drove the workplace a step further than Peter Drucker's views on workers and motivation, then this book signals the next leap forward in human-resource productivity, for a world that has changed inextricably with the advent of the Internet and the explosion of technology. Brady Wilson takes you back to the basics of relating to workers, gives that process context and meaning in today's nanosecond setting, and shows how it can be made to work in any workplace environment.

I have no doubt that this book will juice you to greater insight, creativity, and intelligent energy. Just watch what happens the next time you enter your place of work.

JOHN WRIGHT
Senior Vice President,
Ipsos Reid

Acknowledgments

I am profoundly grateful to my business partner, Alex Somos, who championed this project with unflagging commitment from beginning to end. Alex's creative ideas, practical business sense, and wise advice shaped so much of this book. I have never met a man more thoughtful and loyal than he.

I am also grateful to my friend and colleague Crista Renner. She is Pull Conversation personified. Her ideas and well-crafted questions brought intelligent energy to the table, boosting the book's coherence. Crista is also a brilliant sleuth. Time after time, at the most critical junctures of the writing, she brought forth salient pieces of research.

Loretta Rose was a key player in the formation of this book. She captured much of our initial material on tape and in interviews, channeling my thinking and doing the tough slogging of creating the first draft. Several revisions have come and gone, and most of the book has morphed into a different form, but stories transformed by Loretta from oral to written form are featured throughout. Her intelligence, passion, creativity, and storytelling flair have enriched *Juice* in many ways.

Through his editorial and publishing prowess, Donald G. Bastian of Bastian Books has brought immense value to this book. I am thankful for the day we met.

My thanks also to Sue Krautkramer, Christy Pettit, Rick Boersma, and Dave Loney for helping shape this book through their candid and valuable thoughts during its conception, gestation, and birth.

I am extremely thankful for my wife, who cheerfully gave me the space and time I needed to do this work. Maybe the next one won't take three years, Theresa. Thanks also to Tyler, Katelyn, Mike, Rachel, Adrian, and Alison for their continued interest in the progress of Dad's endless book project.

Many of us are discovering the impact of spirituality on our work. Throughout this process, I have become keenly aware that I could not have completed this task without the creativity, energy, and wisdom that comes from my relationship with God. When I add this to all the friends and family I have acknowledged, I realize just how very fortunate I am.

Introduction

*P*ICTURE yourself looking back over the accomplishments of a stunningly productive day. To what do you attribute your productivity? Your talents didn't change from yesterday to today. Your education, skills, and experience may have grown, but only incrementally. What produced a spike in your performance in such a short time?

The answer is simple: *Your personal energy level.* Not just the raw drive of bulldozer energy, but what we call juice: intelligent energy, the source of focus, flow, passion, and purpose that produces astonishing results.

Energy is the ability to get work done, and one of today's major scientific and technological quests is to discover alternate energy sources to power our vehicles, heat our homes, and fuel our factories. However important this quest may be, there is no place where the production of energy is more important than within us. In so many ways, energy has become the currency of this sped-up, stressed-out, spread-thin, but very exciting new millennium of ours.

Think about your personal energy level for a moment. When you put it together with the energy levels of those you work with, it produces organizational energy. This is where the release of energy really begins to capture our attention. Cultures filled with this kinetic buzz of intelligent energy ignite smart behaviors: people anticipate one another's needs, share information and resources, and leverage one another's efforts. Sustained results are a natural byproduct.

If you are a leader, your job is to guard the energy level of your organization. As you sit at your company's dashboard, there is one gauge you should be checking constantly: your organizational energy gauge. It's even more important than the engagement and retention gauges. Why? Because an employee can be completely engaged yet become depleted in their energy if their core emotional needs are not met. Take care of their energy scores and you will secure their engagement and retention scores as well. The reverse, however, is not necessarily true. The question, then, is, How do we release energy in people?

Imagine our surprise when we discovered that the "new" way of releasing energy is an old way. In fact, we've come to suspect that it's the *only* way that intelligent energy has ever been released: through powerful conversations. Maybe not the type of conversations you are used to, but the kind of conversations that get to the Bigger Reality of a situation.

This book will show you how to uncover the Bigger Reality through what we call Pull Conversation, a blend of inquiry and directness that is perfectly suited to get you to reality.

People have one of two basic orientations in their conversations: push or pull. Those who push their reality onto others trigger a defensiveness that causes their listeners to shut down. Misunderstandings, mistrust, and mistakes typically follow. Those who pull out others' realities generate the kind of understanding that creates trust and high-performing behaviors.

By reading and applying this book, leaders and managers will learn how to pull out the reality of their co-workers and employees. This will earn them the right to pull others into their reality. Between these two realities there is typically a Bigger Reality, lying hidden beneath the surface, at a foundational level. When you are involved in this powerful type of conversation, you will uncover this reality and pull it up to the surface. Once you do that, intelligent energy is released into the situation. What happens next is a magical $1 + 1 = 5$ reaction in which the smartest decisions become apparent and the smartest behaviors become empowered.

In the chapters that follow, you will see the remarkable results that are produced by intelligent energy. You will also see that there is one person who has more capacity to create energy-filled cultures than anyone else. That person is called the leader. The leader sends out a wavelength that others resonate with, whether they realize it or not. Leaders who act as cultural architects create energy-infused environments and end up expanding their leadership influence. This gives them the juice (influence) they need to move people to action.

≈

I am fortunate to work with a passionate group of people. Our company, Juice Inc., exists for one very simple purpose: to co-create cultures where it feels good to work and it's easier to get results. That is why this book has come into existence. After seeing our methods enhance the enjoyment and achievement of our participants, it became apparent to us that this material needed to be offered to the world. As you engage with me in this book, my hope is that *you* will experience this dynamic shift.

I am also fortunate to have had the privilege of working with business leaders and managers from across North America. I will be introducing many of them to you and recognizing how they have released intelligent energy in their work environments.

The sequence of thought in this book is straightforward. Chapter 1 illustrates how conversations release energy. Chapter 2 defines Pull Conversation and shows that while push severs you from others' realities, Pull enables you to pull out others' realities. As

Chapter 3 shows, pulling the reality from others gives you context: the ability to perceive as a sensible whole what others see as disconnected parts. Chapter 4 reveals how to make yourself understood quickly by pulling others into your reality. This leads to an amazing phenomenon, discussed in Chapter 5: how two people or many people in groups can work together to uncover the Bigger Reality.

Although the first five chapters of the book are themselves rich in illustrations from real working life, the rest of the book is even more specific about the practical results of Pull Conversations. It shows how these conversations release energy in organizations, heightening people's output and strengthening relationships. The book wraps up by giving you sixteen practical ways to release intelligent energy in your company through Pull Conversations.

As a bonus, all of the chapters, except the final one, end with a section called "Juice at Home," illustrating the topics of the book in non-business settings. We have a solid rationale for telling these personal stories in a business book. Demonstrating the skills of Pull Conversation at home is the litmus test of the theory – in fact, doing so is often a bigger challenge than demonstrating them at work. And, in any case, for these skills to persist in our behavior at work, they must be practiced at home.

$$\approx$$

My best stuff emerges when I'm with a group of people, helping them work through the issues that are most critical to them. Ironically, here I am interacting with you on the topic of conversation through the medium of paper and ink. I can compensate for the fact that we do not have the luxury of face-to-face conversations by picturing you, the reader, engaging with this material as you sit in your office or home, or even at some vacation spot, perhaps on the beach or on a sailboat. To help you engage with me, I will tell stories throughout this book that will let you in on who I am and how I came to the ideas and practices you are reading about. If you're game, send me your stories of how this material helps you in your work and closest personal relationships. You may reach me at bradywilson@juiceinc.ca.

Conversations Release Energy

Accessing the Power of Pull

*A*large Australian telecommunications company was exploring dialogue and team building. Amanda, a young consultant, was brought in to help Unit B with social mapping, strategic planning, and other processes. The company got more than it bargained for with this consultant. They soon learned that in her work she routinely goes beyond the processes to people. One way she did this, in this assignment, was to start up what she calls the Red Room.

Amanda had the team meet once a month in the red upper room of a funky downtown restaurant, with a standing invitation to anyone in the company who was interested.

This was their oasis for conversation – just conversation. The discussion was loosely guided by Amanda. Sometimes she would kick things off by introducing new tools or ideas that were exciting her and let things proceed from there. But the main point of the Red Room was to get people face to face to say what they really wanted to say, in a safe place of trust and honest exploration. People didn't necessarily even talk about work, just about whatever was important to them. They would spend a whole afternoon in these conversations (and often continue them elsewhere, into the night).

One afternoon Amanda introduced an exercise, created by Loretta Rose (coracle@bserv.com), called the Team Trading Floor. In this exercise, she had team members brainstorm what they needed from one another and things they could provide to one another (work related, relational, family … anything at all). Then they traded among themselves, matching what they needed with what they could give.

The team loved the idea so much that they tried it back at the office. One member had written down that he wanted to learn to dance salsa. To his surprise, "I can teach salsa dancing" was on the list of one of his teammates. He immediately signed an agreement with her for lessons.

A couple of weeks later, Amanda got a call from one of the VPs.

"I want to come to the Red Room," he said.

"Of course!" said Amanda. "The Red Room is open to anyone. You're welcome to come."

"I just never gave it much thought before, but now I'd like to come and see."

"What changed your mind?"

After a long pause, the VP said, "I don't get it; what *is* it you do up there?"

"We just talk."

"I don't get it," he repeated, and Amanda could almost see him shaking his head on the other end of the phone. "Last week I was down to visit Unit B. As I was walking through the cafeteria, two people were dancing salsa. And their unit's income has *doubled* in the past six months! When I ask them how they're pulling that off, all they talk about is the Red Room. What are you *doing* to them in that room?"

Conversations and Energy

What she was doing, or, rather, what everyone in the room was doing, was releasing energy through conversation. The energy flowed personally and even idiosyncratically, which is what had the VP scratching his head. But it also flowed into the everyday processes of the company, creating better results – which is what *really* caught the VP's attention.

Conversation Is Atomic in Nature

An atom is a small thing, but depending on how it is split, it can productively light up the city of Toronto (read nuclear energy) or destructively light up the city of Hiroshima (read atomic bomb).

A conversation is like that. Depending on how it is conducted, it can create large-scale productive results or large-scale negative results. Every conversation is a chance to release either positive or negative energy. A simple performance appraisal can leave employees feeling supercharged and ready to throw themselves back into their work, or deflated and ready to throw in the towel. Every interaction you have with someone is an opportunity to release energy inside them. And energy is very important when it comes to getting things done.

> *Every interaction you have with someone is an opportunity to release energy inside them.*

Feeling the Energy

There are many ways to detect the presence of energy in a work environment. Most of them are things you can see with your eyes. But I still remember the tingle of excitement that prickled up the back of my neck the first time I *heard* the presence of energy.

It was several years ago and I was doing some leadership coaching inside Purolator Courier's central hub operation in Toronto. I was shadowing supervisors on the job to understand exactly what their worlds were like. At first I was overwhelmed, as I saw an operation where twenty-four trailers simultaneously unloaded thousands of parcels onto a series of conveyor belts, with twenty-four belts converging on one massive sorting area up high in the sweltering hot building. This was the primary belt where the parcels were sorted onto secondary belts and redirected to many load-out docks all around the plant.

As I moved toward the primary belt I heard a sound that made my pulse quicken. How can I describe it? It was a deep-chested rumbling chant that rose and fell and resounded even over the deafening din of the conveyor belts: O-O-O-H – o-o-o-h – O-O-O-H, O-O-O-H – o-o-o-h – O-O-O-H, O-O-O-H – o-o-o-h – O-O-O-H.

I asked if I could see what was happening up on the primary belt. As I climbed the stairs I saw a lineup of chanting men working together like a massive muscle machine. They were pulling boxes off an endless steel slide and lifting them onto conveyor belts at different heights.

Each worker hoisted boxes of fifty to sixty pounds each every few seconds. The pace was relentless. No matter how many boxes they lifted, the slide remained packed. The plant processed as many as 150,000 parcels every twenty-four hours.

I noticed a guy in a white shirt and tie weaving in and out of the men. I learned that his name was Dino. He was keeping the energy flowing, bantering away with his men, asking them how it was going, pitching in to help here, un-jamming a bottleneck there.

It was obvious that the men were performing at a highly productive level, but what really caught my attention was the raw kinetic energy created by this amazing supervisor. There was a hum, a buzz, a spark of excitement flowing all the way up and down the primary belt. The word that comes to me when I witness this type of energy working in a team is juice. This team was juiced to be doing what they were doing, even though it was one of the toughest jobs in the organization.

I later learned that in this plant of 600 employees, with a significantly transient workforce, attendance was a brutal problem for the supervisors. Not for Dino, though. His men showed up regularly, and their productivity was outstanding. Somehow he had discovered the secret of releasing a feeling of energy in his employees, and this energy was enabling them to move smoothly through a mountain of work every night.

Interviewing and watching Dino, I discovered what his secret was: he showed respect for his men by engaging them in frequent face-to-face conversations. He was leveraging what Edward

Hallowell in the *Harvard Business Review* (Jan.-Feb.1999) dubs "The Human Moment at Work."

> The human moment has two prerequisites: people's physical presence and their emotional and intellectual attention ... To make the human moment work, you have to set aside what you're doing, put down the memo you were reading, disengage from your laptop, abandon your daydream, and focus on the person you are with. Usually when you do that, the other person will *feel the energy and respond in kind.* Together, you quickly create a *force field of exceptional power.* [emphasis mine]

Investing in those short human moments was paying Dino back handsomely. He spent very little time arranging for temps, grinding through discipline issues, and resolving employee complaints.

Energy Is What Gets Work Done

Look at your own productivity over a thirty-day period. Your talents don't change much from one day to the next. Your knowledge and experience grow incrementally. But the one thing that can create a spike in your productivity from one day to the next is your personal energy level.

The one thing that can create a spike in your productivity from one day to the next is your personal energy level.

Take your personal energy level and combine it with the energy levels of your co-workers. This produces your organizational energy level. I have had the privilege of working with some of the finest organizations in North America. You can feel a kinetic buzz as you make contact with some of their departments or teams. Perhaps this helps make sense of our high-school physics definition of energy: *energy is the ability to do work.*

Energy Unlocks Effort

When employees feel energized, they love to offer their best stuff: their discretionary effort. Discretionary effort is a willingness to go above and beyond the call of duty to perform tasks and exemplify attitudes that benefit the company.

Several years ago I heard about an intriguing research project in which employees were asked, "If you were to put in 15% more effort, do you think your manager would notice?" The employees' general response was, "No, my manager isn't that tuned into my daily reality to notice anything like that."

The researchers then asked the employees, "If you were to put in 15% *less* effort, do you think your manager would notice?" The employees' response was no again.

If this dynamic is true, it means that some employees have up to 30% more discretionary effort to offer but aren't feeling energized to offer it. What percent of your employees do you think could be offering more? Engagement studies reveal that only 20% of the North American workforce are highly engaged. Of the remaining 80%, 60% are moderately engaged and another 20% are disengaged.

When Employees Are Energized ...

What if you could enable 10% of your disengaged employees to become moderately engaged? How would that change your reality? What if you could enable 10% of your moderately engaged employees to become highly engaged? And, finally, what if you could free up 10% of your disengaged employees to pursue a career with your arch-competitor? When employees are energized, they offer their discretionary effort and that changes your reality as a leader. There's less turnover, higher productivity, higher revenues, decreased costs, and greater profitability.

Intelligent – Not Raw – Energy

But high performance doesn't just come from raw energy. Even a bulldozer has that. High performance comes from *intelligent energy*, a sense of:

- Focus
- Flow
- Passion
- Purpose
- Drive

We're not talking about whipping up the troops with motivational froth. We're talking about engaging your workforce with the kind of conversation that produces an intelligent, cohesive, highly aligned energy. Pull Conversation, the central concept of this book, is a specific type of conversation that best releases this kind of organizational energy, one in which a leader does the hard work of pulling out the reality of their employees. The following story illustrates how this type of conversation works. It also shows the type of energy and results that are released when leaders pull instead of push.

> *We're talking about engaging your workforce with the kind of conversation that produces an intelligent, cohesive, highly aligned energy.*

Pull Conversations in Action

Energizing a Turnaround

David was the VP of marketing in an international food company and he needed a breakthrough. A Canadian by birth, he had more than proved himself during his tenure in both Canada and United States. But now he found himself severely challenged. He had been parachuted into an underperforming UK branch with a clear mandate from world headquarters: "Turn this division around and get us results."

Whether it was because of UK culture, personalities, organizational history, or some other reason, David's branch just wasn't hitting its numbers. He had pushed hard for two years but it seemed that his marketing leadership team (MLT) was unwilling to be on the hook with him for results. When he wasn't there, they took very little initiative, even failing to hold leadership meetings. The rumblings from head office were getting more and more ominous.

With stress mounting, David enlisted the help of Mitch Fairrais, a colleague of mine from On the Mark, a Toronto-based training company. On the Mark and Juice formed a team and set about trying to help David achieve his breakthrough.

After a day of training the marketing team how to pull out

(understand) one another's realities in conversation, we settled into day two: using Pull Conversation to solve the substantive trust and commitment issues of David and his MLT.

Mitch and I believed that if David and his team could learn to pull understanding out of each other rather than trying to push their understanding onto each other, they could resolve the situation. For this to happen, David first had to pull from his team.

We guaranteed David, based on our experience of situations like his, that if he stepped into his leadership team's world and pulled out their reality, they would reciprocate and seek to understand his reality as well.

The MLT's Reality

As mentioned, on day one we used a series of experiences to teach the entire marketing leadership team the skills of Pull Conversation. We focused on inquiry: the ability to step into another person's world to see their reality the way they see it.

On day two, David was on the hot seat with a mandate to pull out his team's reality. It proved to be extremely challenging for him and he almost jettisoned the process, but to his credit, he pressed on. He stepped into their worlds and pulled out their thoughts, feelings, and assumptions. As he did so, he made an alarming discovery: his MLT saw him as a mercenary who wanted results with no concern for the human cost.

David fought his instinctive desire to defend himself and push his world onto them. He swallowed hard as they shared their perception of him as someone who didn't value their British culture, as someone who was only in it for the short haul, a manager who was taking the North American approach of dangling a carrot in front of them to get them to perform.

With help, David resisted the temptation to justify himself and repeatedly sought to step into their world and reflect back what they were saying in his own words.

Slowly, almost imperceptibly, the group began to feel understood and their capacity to hear David's viewpoint grew. Finally, at about the three-quarter mark of the second day, a clearly discernible shift occurred in the room.

One of David's leaders asked, "When you can't be here, we should still meet and keep things moving."

Someone else said, "Maybe we can help find ways to make people feel recognized and rewarded."

Others jumped in with, "Yes, and how can we get on the hook with you and give you the commitment you need?"

We witnessed the result of David's Pull approach: the release of intelligence and energy in the group.

A feeling of electricity was now coursing through the room. Mitch and I were optimistic as we witnessed the result of David's Pull approach: the release of intelligence and energy in the group. The other eleven were now turning toward David, asking him about himself and beginning to pull out his reality.

David's Reality

David and his family had paid a high price for this job, and he wasn't at all sure that it was worth it. He had never mentioned the personal costs to his team. As he saw it, he'd made choices, and they were his to own. He believed it would be cowardly to try to get his staff to understand what he was dealing with.

Now, however, he realized that he had to pull his team into his reality and help them understand his world. Because he had pulled out his team's reality, he had created capacity in them to do the same for him. He had earned the right to speak and they were ready to listen.

He told the group the story of a time when he'd been hurrying to pick up his young son Matthew from school. As he closed his office door, an employee stopped him with some questions and concerns. David answered as briefly as he could, then said he needed to go because his five-year-old son was waiting. The employee followed him into the elevator, continuing the discussion down several floors and through the parking lot to David's car.

David, aware that he was now late, tried to get into his car, but the employee kept talking. David was growing more anxious by the second but felt as the leader of the company he must listen to this employee, who clearly felt she had to get her need met, right then. When he was finally able to extricate himself, he drove all the way to Matthew's school at twice the speed limit, his stomach knotted with anxiety, his life in danger as he roared and wove through traffic. He *had* to get to Matthew; but he also *had* to be there for his staff. It was a no-win situation.

He also shared that he and his family had moved to a new country without any friends or family or social network to support them. His team members had made no effort to make his wife and him feel included, he said. The team hadn't invited them to their homes or social functions.

David was very direct as he spoke out his reality to his staff. He could see they hadn't viewed him as a multifaceted person with a family and personal issues, but simply as a leader who was supposed to meet their needs. There was a lot of discomfort in the room as he talked, but this was part of David's reality and therefore part of the whole group's reality. Their reality as a group needed to be bigger. They needed to understand each other's contexts.

All of us in the room saw something powerful happen that day. As a leader, David used a combination of pulling out his team's reality and pulling them into his reality. But it mattered which one he did first. Pull Conversation is based on the simple hypothesis that if you do an effective job of pulling out someone's reality and making them feel deeply understood, they will reciprocate by trying to pull out your reality. This willingness to reciprocate is not restricted to understanding. When we feel respected by someone, it is easier for us to respect them. And when we feel trusted by someone, it is easier for us to trust them. This is known as the Law of Psychological Reciprocity. Robert K. Greenleaf, in *The Leader as Servant*, defines it this way: "People are impelled to return to you the feelings you create in them."

The Saint of Reciprocity

The famous prayer of St. Francis of Assisi primes us to line up our behaviors with the law of reciprocity:

> *Grant that we may not so much seek*
> *To be consoled as to console;*
> *To be understood as to understand;*
> *To be loved as to love.*

Feeling understood is one of our primal needs as human beings. Meet this crucial need for others and they will respond by meeting it for you. There are exceptions, of course. However, having helped hundreds of leaders, managers, and employees work through thorny situations and achieve productive outcomes, I can confidently say that most people will try to understand you if you seek to understand them first.

A Bigger Reality Emerges

When two parties have vastly different views on an issue, there is often an underlying Bigger Reality that is invisible to both of them. I have learned that the key to releasing energy and achieving results is uncovering, or pulling out, that Bigger Reality.

Now that David had done the work of pulling out the reality of his leadership team and pulling them into his reality, he was able to move forward to uncover the Bigger Reality that was hidden to everyone. To do this, it was necessary to find the common ground that existed between their seemingly polarized viewpoints.

A question I have found to be useful in identifying the common ground is, "What is it we both want here that would allow us to move forward?" This is where David and his team began to apply their focus.

David and his leadership team discovered that they both wanted to produce great results. They both wanted to retain the distinctive elements of UK culture. They both prized family over work. There was ample common ground here from which a Bigger Reality could emerge.

Discoveries from Getting to Common Ground

Getting to common ground releases intelligence and open thinking. Here are some of the discoveries that came to the surface as a result of the progress David and his team were making:

- David realized, "This team really does want to get on the hook and pump out great results."
- The team realized, "David isn't here to destroy our culture – and he's not just here for a one-year stint to bolster his CV."
- The team also realized, "We've been guilty of doing to David

exactly what we accused him of wanting to do to us. We've been jeopardizing his family life for the sake of getting our work needs met."

Uncovering these discoveries was a breakthrough. David and his team now understood each other's motives, how to meet each other's unique emotional needs, how to become one, and, therefore, how to move forward. These discoveries were instrumental in uncovering the Bigger Reality, and when they achieved this, working together and reaching their goals became very simple.

The Bigger Reality

What was the Bigger Reality? It was a solid belief, a firm conclusion, embedded in a sense of possibility: "We can do this. We can achieve great results without working obscene hours and destroying our culture. We can work together in a different way – a radically different way. What might we be able to achieve if we dropped the suspicion and the resistance and replaced them with focus and collaboration?"

> "What might we be able to achieve if we dropped the suspicion and the resistance and replaced them with focus and collaboration?"

One might well respond, "What sort of Bigger Reality is that? It doesn't seem magical at all to me." Perhaps, but consider that when this team was mired in suspicion and mistrust, the prevailing mindset was, "We either adopt the insane North American work ethic and kiss goodbye to our culture or we fail to hit our numbers and kiss goodbye to our jobs." This type of mindset does not typically produce much intelligent energy.

This simple but powerful Bigger Reality had an instant effect on David and his team. Intelligent energy began to flow and high-performing behaviors began to emerge. David's team got on the hook for results. They began to collaborate freely, share resources, and leverage one another's efforts.

Some may well say, "My day is way too packed to do this Pull Conversation stuff. It takes too long. I've got no choice but to push!" But consider this: by pulling, *David was able to achieve in two* short days what he had been unable to accomplish in two years of *dogged pushing*. Because the Bigger Reality produces a magical 1+1 = 5 effect, it's worth whatever you have to expend to pull it out.

And the powerful thing about this breakthrough is that it wasn't

> *And the powerful thing about this breakthrough is that it wasn't a one-time affair. The experience changed the team.*

a one-time affair. The experience changed the team. We checked back with David several times in the ensuing months and years. His team began to achieve unprecedented financial results. In fact, they doubled their growth in one year. And David was finally able to take a long-deserved holiday. Why? Because he felt complete confidence in his team while he was gone.

The point of this story is simple. Conversation, done the right way, releases intelligent energy; intelligent energy produces smart behaviors; and smart behaviors produce sustained results. You get to choose: two years of push with no results or two days of Pull with lasting results. What you'll see in this book is that the quickest way to get to sustained results is to pull out the Bigger Reality. As hyped as this may sound, we've witnessed that Pull truly is a 1 + 1 = 5 equation.

Pull Conversation: The Model

That brings us to a fuller statement of the Pull Conversation Model, which is the essence of all the chapters to follow. This model works in all situations, whether personal or business, but we will use the language of business predominantly throughout this book. Our primary audience is the manager or leader working with a team.

Portions of the model will appear in the next several chapters as we concentrate on various steps that it lays out. Fuller statements of the steps follow each iteration of the model.

Following is how the model works, reading from the bottom of the page to the top. Note that the steps in this model are filled out in detail below this first use of the model in this book.

Pull Conversation™ Model

6 **Sustained Results**
- Revenue
- Quality
- Loyalty
- Innovation
- Speed
- Safety
- Retention
- Profit

Targeted Results

5 **High-Performing Behaviors**
- Anticipating each other's needs
- Sharing resources & information
- Leveraging each other's efforts
- Collaborating and synergizing
- Covering each other's backs

Aligned Actions

4 **Intelligent Energy**
- Focus
- Flow
- Passion
- Purpose
- Drive

Smart Decisions

3 **Pull out the Bigger Reality**
- Bring your two worlds together to find the common ground
- Look for a Bigger Reality to emerge — a solution that works for both of you
- Sum it up in your own words

*Common Ground
The Bigger Reality*

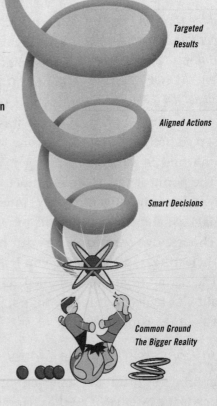

2 **Pull them into your reality**
- Invite them into your world
- Help them see your reality
- Ask them to reflect back what they've understood

Your Reality

1 **Pull out their reality**
- Step into their world
- See and feel their reality
- Reflect it back in your own words

Their Reality

1 *Pull Out Their Reality*

   A Step into their world: Temporarily set your judgments and fears aside and inquire deeply into the way they see things.

   B See their reality: Using the power of your mind's eye, see what it's like to be them in this situation. Pull out the assumptions that they are operating from.

   C Reflect back what you've understood in your own words to ensure that they feel understood.

2 *Pull Them into Your Reality*

   A Invite them into your world: Make them curious by using the power of story and finding language that makes it easy for them to relate to you.

   B Help them see your reality: Speak your truth productively and draw out the assumptions that you are operating from.

   C Ask them to reflect back what they've understood.

3 *Pull Out the Bigger Reality*

   A Bring your two worlds together to find the common ground. Do this by asking, "What is it we both want here?"

   B Look for a Bigger Reality to emerge. Ask yourselves, "Is there a Bigger Reality here that would allow us to move forward?"

   C Sum it up in your own words.

4 *Intelligent Energy*

Getting to the Bigger Reality releases intelligent energy. People's attention becomes focused. They move into a flow state where they are completely engrossed in their work. There is a strong sense of passion as they do what they are juiced to do. They are deeply in touch with the purpose of their work. This creates an empowering sense of drive that fuels high-performing behaviors.

5 *High-Performing Behaviors*

Intelligent energy fuels the types of behaviors you dream of as a leader. Employees begin to understand and anticipate one another's needs. They freely share resources and information. They leverage one another's efforts, investing moments of effort that save hours of time for their co-workers. They collaborate and synergize. They have one another's backs.

6 *Sustained Results*

High-performing behaviors produce sustained results such as increased revenue, greater quality, customer loyalty, brilliant innovations and speed to market, *and* improved safety, retention, and bottom-line profits.

How to Pull Out Their Reality

Like David, you will have to do everything in your power to inquire into the other person's or group's reality. You will have to step out of your world and let go of your assumptions, judgments, and fears and listen intently for a significant chunk of time in order to step into their world. You will have to use the power of your mind's eye to see their reality – to picture what it is like to be them in this situation. Then you will have to reflect back what they are saying in your own words to demonstrate that you really understand what they are saying.

How to Pull Them into Your Reality

When you pull out the other person's reality, you will build capacity and desire within them to understand and care about what you have to say. It's at this point that you pull them into your reality by sharing a story like the one David did of racing to pick up his son, Matthew. Use stories to invite others into your world. The graphic image of David weaving through traffic at breakneck speeds to get to his son had a lasting impact on his team.

Speaking your truth productively in a very direct, respectful way will enable others to see and feel your reality. After you have done this, help them reflect it back to you until:

- They really get what you are trying to say.
- They don't walk away with anything you aren't trying to say.

Conversation: An Organizational Operating System

Conversation is the operating system of your organization. What is an operating system? Let's say you needed to create a PowerPoint presentation. You can't communicate with the PowerPoint application in your computer without a translator. In many computers, that translator is Windows. Windows is simply an operating system that enables an application like PowerPoint to store and display itself through your hardware.

In the same way, the needs of your organization and the applications that will meet those needs require an operating system to link them and enable them. Conversation is that operating system. For instance, your organization needs to receive orders from your customers. The "application" that will produce that work is an order-entry process. The operating system that links the customer's order to that process is a conversation between a call taker and the customer. The quality of that conversation dictates the quality of service to your customers.

Ultimately, every facet of your organization runs off this operating system of conversation: recruitment runs off hiring conversations; performance runs off training conversations; and revenue runs off sales conversations.

Conversation translates employees' talents to the needs of the organization. Conversation translates employees' talents to the needs of the organization.

What percent of your day do you spend conversing? Edward Shaw, a corporate training expert, makes some interesting observations in his book *The Six Pillars of Reality-Based Training*. According to Shaw, studies show that in white-collar workplaces, people spend their time doing just four main activities:

Conversing	*60–95 %*
Reading	*20–50 %*
Writing	*10–45 %*
Thinking/planning	*0–15 %*

If conversation is the activity you spend up to 95% of your day doing, then every minute or dollar you spend fine-tuning this operating system will go a long way toward leveraging your effectiveness. As the following stories illustrate, when the operating system of conversation is undervalued and underused, you end up weakening all of your other systems.

Poor Communication: Pull the Plug

In 2001, a grocery giant pulled the plug on a $49-million IT implementation. That's stunning. Picture yourself walking away from an investment of that magnitude just to cut your losses. And this company is by no means alone. A litany of thousands of other IT heartbreaks could be cited if one had the time and the stomach for it. Thousands? Yes, in their *Chaos Report*, 1994, the Standish Group estimated that $81 billion would be wasted on cancelled software projects the following year. In their *Extreme Chaos* report of 2001, they reported that in the year prior, 23% of the 30,000 technology-driven implementations failed completely and another 49% were "*challenged* – a term encompassing cost and time overruns and missing features."

What is one of the key reasons that IT implementations fail? The same report attributed the failures to poor communication skills of the project manager and primary users.

I could cite scores of other such examples. I have personally witnessed organizations investing many thousands of dollars on Balanced Scorecards, 360° leadership surveys, and performance-management systems that only delivered a fraction of what they promised. And the common denominator that truncated the effectiveness of every one of these programs was the lack of skilled face-to-face conversation. For example:

- A leader gets 360° feedback indicating that she isn't providing inspirational leadership. Instead of going face to face and pulling from each employee what specific adjustments she could make to meet their specific needs for inspiration, she makes her own guesses about how to be more inspiring. Her modified behaviors after the 360° process are at best a good guess and at worst inappropriate and damaging.
- An elaborate performance-management system is implemented

that puts managers in the role of populating multiple screens of performance data. In the process, little meaningful conversation occurs to identify the obstacles to performance or inspire the employee to higher levels of performance.

- A wellness program has been kicked off in your organization. Because there's no "budge-factor" on the results employees have to achieve, the only way to reduce spillover between work and home is to give employees more job control and flextime. This automatically opens the door to chaos as employees who can't work from home start resenting the ones who can, and employees who have to be at work at core times compare themselves with the ones who get to take advantage of flextime. If managers are not equipped to work through the chaos and have the tough conversations, your wellness program is going to be a little sickly.

Conversation and Goal Clarity

Smart leaders find innovative ways to use the operating system of conversation to drive the most important applications of their business. Here, from *Communication World*, July–August 2004, is a unique story of a scooter company that begins every day with conversations designed to focus the entire organization on the goals that will move the business forward.

Huddles begin each day at 8:30 A.M. Within an hour, every employee will have communicated up, down and across the entire company.

For 15 minutes, frontline employees meet as a department with their managers. Then managers leave for a second 15-minute huddle with their directors. Directors then meet with vice presidents. Finally, vice presidents huddle with the CEO and finish by 9:30 A.M.

People in the field participate by telephone. The most any one person dedicates to the process is 30 minutes, and it gives everyone a daily connection to the CEO.

They talk about the day's business priorities, anticipate problems and put rumors to rest. Each department has quarterly goals, and at every huddle, each employee states what he or she will do that day toward achieving goals.

"We go around the group, which may have as many as 10 people, for each person to give his or her number one focus for today, given the clear quarterly focus," says Jeff Austin, human resources vice president. "It's a chance to talk about any bottleneck you think you might encounter." Managers address bottlenecks at that time or in the next-level huddle. Managers also ask each individual if he or she completed yesterday's number one goal.

By identifying what an employee can accomplish today, and what an employee accomplished yesterday, quarterly goals break into doable chunks. "It's a great exchange of information and sharing time. Sometimes people will get into a side discussion that turns out to be critical," says Debbie Featherston, vice president of PeopleWerks – Celebrations and Communications.

What Are We Really Saying Here?

- It is the release of intelligent energy that produces results for your organization.
- By pulling, it is possible to achieve in two days what you couldn't achieve in two years of pushing.
- Conversation is the operating system that energizes and runs all your other systems.
- When trying to get people to buy in, invest time and pull out their reality before pulling them into your reality.

Want to Make This Happen?

- Create your company's **Red Room**.
- Get your supervisors creating more **human moments** with their employees.
- Get your leaders pulling out the realities of their leadership teams to help them **get on the hook** for results.
- Ensure that Pull Conversation, performed face to face, is integrated with the systems you have already invested in (Balanced Score Card, 360° Measurement, Performance Review, Wellness Program).
- Implement fifteen-minute huddle relays.

Juice at Home

Marked for Life

I remember the conversation that marked me for life. When I was thirty-nine, my dad contracted bone cancer. He was lying on what turned out to be his deathbed. The air was heavy with meaning – not the time for light talk. Dad turned to me and talked about how death was close beside him.

For all kinds of reasons that would take up too much space and time to describe, I could never really understand that my dad loved me or was proud of me. He had a hard time conveying his feelings and I had a hard time believing I was lovable or worthy of his pride. I spent many frustrating years trying to win his approval; I even ended up following in his footsteps into the optical industry (he was an optometrist), doing everything I could to make him believe that I was worthy of his love.

I had never invested the energy to understand my dad's reality. But as I sat beside him in those moments, I wanted to understand him more than anything. There was something inside me that wanted to pull out all the understanding I could. I was a thirty-nine-year-old vacuum that needed filling in a very big way.

I began to pull out my dad's reality. I asked him how the pain was. I asked him what it was like to be so close to death. I asked him if he was afraid. His lip quivered and he nodded, saying, "Who in their right mind would think they are good enough to get into God's heaven?" There was a pause, and he said, "But I have faith." He looked at me and said, "You have to have faith."

But those weren't the words that marked me for life. I knew that faith in God was crucial. It was what he said next that left an imprint on me.

He spoke a simple message – words I had never been able to understand: "I love you and I'm proud of you." Weighty words landing on a soft heart make a deep imprint. In a moment of instant clarity, I was vaulted from twisted perceptions to reality, from misunderstanding to understanding, from self-doubt to confidence, and from "I feel like a failure" to "Maybe I can succeed."

How did that moment happen? My hunger to understand my dad made me want to pull out his reality. When he saw my receptivity and my need, he pulled me into his reality. This dynamic of the need to understand and the need to be understood caused us to turn together. I turned toward my dad and pulled out his reality. He turned toward me and pushed out his reality. Turning together created a life-changing conversation. (Interestingly enough, the word *conversation* means just that: *to turn together.*)

But we went beyond just turning together. In this brief moment we stepped into each other's worlds and experienced each other's realities. When I stepped into my dad's world, I felt what he felt: "This is my last chance to let my son know that I love him and I'm proud of him." As for me, feeling this reality for the first time recalibrated my beliefs: faulty beliefs were replaced with reliable ones. As Dad stepped into my world, he could see that I was finally getting what he wanted to give me all along – a sense of his love and blessing. Seeing each other's realities made the way for a Bigger Reality to emerge.

> *Unity is one of the primary goals of communication.*

I believe unity is one of the primary goals of communication. If you separate the word *communication* and put it together from back to front, you come up with a definition that goes like this: communication is *the action of becoming one with.* If that definition is accurate, it's easy to see why conversation is so vital to communication. It's only in turning together that we can become one with another person. In those moments of deep communication, I finally felt one with my dad.

This pivotal conversation released *juice* inside me: an intelligent energy that came from having some of my deepest needs met. An energy that came from the belief that I could finally become successful – that I was worthy of my dad's pride. That energy still empowers and juices me today, nearly a decade later, enabling me to achieve results in areas I never could before.

The Logic of Pull Conversations

Creating Capacity in Your Listeners

*I*N Chapter 1 we saw how conversation releases energy. But only a certain kind of conversation releases intelligent energy: Pull Conversation. We witnessed how Pull Conversation produced a dramatic turnaround in David's UK marketing team. Now it's time to unpack how and why Pull works. Let's take a look at the logic of Pull.

Push or Pull?

Every July I return to Manitoulin Island in Lake Huron to the cottage where I spent the summers of my youth. It's not all fun and games up north. Last year we had to replace the wiring between two of the cottages. Because the new wire was going to be buried, the job entailed running a thick electrical wire through a plastic hose that would protect the wire underground.

How to get 140 feet of wire through 140 feet of plastic hose was the challenge. Mike, the hardware store guy, had offered some advice, but it seemed far-fetched and much too time-consuming. My brother Tim and I decided to try what we thought would be a faster and easier method.

First, we uncoiled the wire and stretched it out in a straight line along the beach. Then we tried pushing the wire through the hose. What we thought would be a relatively simple process proved futile. Although the wire was stiff, the friction proved to be too much, getting things to the point where we could no longer push the wire at all.

What to do next? We thought of taking the wire and the hose and hanging them over the edge of nearby East Bluff. Maybe gravity would overcome the friction and the wire would slowly fall through the hose. But it would take a lot of work to roll up the wire and the hose, drive it up to the bluff, unroll it over the edge, slide the wire through the hose (which we weren't sure would work), roll the hose back up, and drive it back to the lake.

Mike the hardware guy's method was beginning to look more and more attractive, despite the fact that it would require significant up-front work.

Tim took a little piece of a plastic bag and tied a roll of fishing line onto it. I stuck the piece of plastic bag into one end of the hose and Tim went to the other end and stuck a small vacuum cleaner over the end. He turned on the vacuum cleaner and before we knew it, the suction had pulled the fishing line through the hose and to his end.

We then used the fishing line to pull a sturdy string through the hose. Once the string was through, we attached it to the electric wire. We all watched with amazement as I was able to walk along the beach, pulling the thick wire through the hose quickly and easily.

The lesson was embarrassingly clear to us: when it comes to getting something flexible through a conduit, pulling works a lot better than pushing. Pulling reduces unnecessary friction and enables you to get something through in a shorter time and with less stress.

We had defaulted to a push first approach because we believed that it would take too long to pull. We ended up wasting all the time we spent pushing, in the end being forced to invest the time on the pull approach anyway.

Do You Push First?

When I was with Eagle's Flight, one of North America's foremost training companies, I conducted hands-on research in my sessions with people from organizations across North America. Our statistics showed something very interesting about the various simulations that we conducted with the people we were training: *two-thirds* of them take a *push* approach when they want to make themselves understood.

We conducted an exercise framed within a real-estate story. See if you can figure it out.

> A couple purchased a home in one city for $360,000. The wife was offered a promotion that entailed working out of head office, 100 miles away. The couple loved their new home and the wife was loath to commute 100 miles twice a day. Should she accept the promotion or not? They decided to put the house up on the market for $10,000 more than they bought it for. If it sold, that would be their sign that she was supposed to take the new job.
>
> The very next day, an eager young couple bought the house from them for the asking price of $370,000. They packed up their kids and went to buy another house close to head office. The house that appealed to them most was a bit more expensive – they ended up paying $380,000 for it.
>
> Six months later, the kids were complaining about missing their friends and their teachers. The husband hadn't found another job yet and the wife was getting sick of the politics at head office. They decided to put the house up for sale for $390,000. If it sold, they would move back home.
>
> It sold the very next day for $390,000.

At this point, we say to the participants, "This couple is about to get back into their vehicle and move back to their home city. Did they make money, lose money, or break even? If they made or lost money, how much did they make or lose? And just to keep it simple, you don't have to take into consideration any of the legal fees, real estate fees, or moving expenses."

Typically, a portion of the group firmly believes that the couple broke even. Another portion is just as sure that they made $10,000. Another is persuaded that they made $20,000. Yet another says, "It's simple. They made $30,000." Other participants have varying answers. What do you believe the answer is?

At this point, we say to the group, "Your mission now is to try to get on the same page and it would be good if it was the right page. Go and talk to people from a different group. Your task is to make yourself understood in the best way possible."

What happens next is truly interesting to witness. As people try to make their point of view understood, their natural conversation styles naturally come to the surface. Try this for yourself. Show this real estate problem to a friend, colleague, or family member and see if you can get on the same page as to what the right answer is.

We do this for four rounds, or four quarters, if you will. At the end, the group is typically still divided, with people in at least two or three camps. (For the solution to this problem, you may go to www.juiceinc.ca/buyandsell.)

We then ask them, "Think back to the interactions you've just had. What percentage of the people you interacted with pulled out your rationale before asking you to understand theirs? What percentage pushed their rationale on you before trying to understand yours? And what percentage acquiesced – simply giving in to your point of view without trying to advocate their own?"

After polling thousands of people, the results show that when North Americans are trying to get to understanding, 66% of them push, 23% acquiesce, and only 10% pull.

When North Americans are trying to get to understanding, 66% of them push, 23% acquiesce, and only 10% pull.

This means that the chances are at least two to one (66% to 33%) that the people around you are pushing their reality onto you rather than attempting to pull out your reality. And the chances are also two to one that, unless you are exceptional, you're pushing, too. (Our findings mesh with the research of Jack Carew, who studied 30,000 sales professionals and discovered that in any sales interaction the odds are two to one that "the orientation of the salesperson is inwardly focused." (Go to www.carew.com/The Odds Are Factor.)

Look around your professional and personal worlds. Is that what you see? Imagine it otherwise. Imagine what it would be like to walk into a meeting where everybody was committed to a Pull approach. Imagine what it would be like to have conversations with your spouse or teenager or friends where each side tried to outdo the other in pulling the other person's reality out.

Why Does Pull Work Best?

In the 1950s, Toyota shifted manufacturing from a push to a Pull mindset as they began to pull resources into the assembly line as needed, rather than stockpiling huge inventories of parts. It wasn't long before marketing organizations began to adopt the Pull methodology. Media have shifted to a Pull approach within the past decade. In several sectors, people are discovering that Pull works better than push.

When I ask participants, "What's the best way to make yourself understood: to push, pull, or acquiesce?" a full 95% respond, "Pull works best." I always say, "I believe you, but sell this to me. Why do you believe it works best?" Here's what they say:

- *Pull* reduces the other person's defensiveness and increases respect and trust, making them receptive and willing to understand you.
- *Pull* enables you to understand the other person's conversation style. This enables you to frame your message in a way that's easy for them to understand and relate to.
- If there is a block or error in the other person's thinking, *Pull* shows you exactly where the point of departure is. Understanding this helps you discover the best way to get them back on the path of logic.
- If you need the other person to buy into your point of view rather than just give cognitive assent to it, *Pull* does a better job than push of getting them on board.

- The solution may not be either yours or theirs but a hybrid of the two. If you *Pull*, you make sure that you aren't forfeiting a valuable piece of the equation.
- If your own logic is wrong, *Pull* will expose where you've gone off the path and keep you from embarrassing yourself unnecessarily.

The Push Culture

The dynamics of the wire and hose story play themselves out in organizations and families every day.

Let's say I'm heading into a meeting. I have a strong point of view about the topic up for discussion. I believe my job is to push my point of view out to others until they get it. When I begin to push my viewpoint, my team members start getting defensive. I sense their resistance and it triggers in me a need to push more. I have to get my point through to them. They become even more resistant and less receptive to my ideas. Two team members outright stonewall me. Three or four others nod politely and indicate that they will seriously consider my point of view.

Logic, Passion Not Sufficient

Here's a statement you can take to the bank: *People will tolerate your conclusions and act on their own.* You may be able to get people to nod their heads by the force of your logic or the strength of your passion. But when they walk away to take action, they will act on their own conclusions, not yours.

Here is one of many situations I have witnessed that are emblematic of our push culture.

Push Stalls an Implementation

Steve and some of his key leaders are about to go into a meeting with their management team. Steve is the leader of a chemical plant and he wants to implement SAP, a technology solution that promises to integrate a broad range of organizational processes and make his people more efficient. Steve and his leadership cadre feel passionate about their point of view. It's critical to them that the managers understand it. With so much at stake, Steve believes that the best approach is to present the merits of his ideas to others with strength, to passionately push his point of view on the others until they "get it."

So he lays it out to his management team, and, rallying all his enthusiasm, outlines all the facts and stats of why SAP is the best way to go. At the end of his presentation, he asks a perfunctory, "Any questions, concerns, or ideas?" but every manager knows that Steve is not interested in feedback. He just wants to get this thing implemented, now.

Sixteen weeks later, SAP is mired in employee-relations problems. Despite the leadership team's encouragements, ultimatums, and even threats, people seem unclear about the process and hand-offs are not happening effectively. It seems there is not enough *group will* to get the project over the inevitable bumps. Worst of all, the employees who are supposed to be benefiting from SAP are overtly or covertly finding ways to sabotage the new system. Spotty compliance has created a mess made up of the old and new: an ugly hybrid of reports, processes, and systems that are practically useless because they offer neither the comfort of the old system nor the ease and accuracy of the new.

At this point, Steve calls for help. Group dialogues are facilitated between him, his managers, and his employees. Steve and his leaders receive coaching on a few critical skills:

- How to set aside their own agenda and inquire into the concerns and goals of their managers and employees without judgment or defensiveness.
- How to step into their employees' worlds to see their reality.
- How to reflect back the essence of what they are saying in his own words so they feel completely understood and respected.

As Steve begins to pull, he discovers some concerns and objections that have some serious validity – concerns and objections that left unaddressed will sink the entire process. For example, he discovers that he had failed to understand the needs and the fears of his end users. He had mistakenly assumed that operators would immediately see the benefit of the new system and wholeheartedly embrace the change. As Stone, Patton, and Heen say in *Difficult Conversations*, "People almost never change without feeling understood first."

> "People almost never change without feeling understood first."

Steve had completely underestimated their paranoia about touching a computer. Seeing this reality helped him understand that the training process for the operators was not only too short, it was rolled out in a way that was guaranteed to turn them off.

As Steve begins to make his employees feel understood, they admit their own part in the failure that they had not really done an honest job of understanding the leadership team's desire to make their jobs easier.

Like Tim and me in the wire and hose story, Steve believed that there was no time to pull and so defaulted to push. Pushing cost him dearly. Much of the energy expended in the first sixteen weeks was wasted. In the end, although Steve resorted to the Pull approach, it took him months to overcome the cynicism, lack of trust, and reluctance that he had created by pushing first.

Let me ask you, do your implementations grind to a halt because the ideas aren't smart enough or because they run out of energy? Most organizations don't lack good ideas, they lack the intelligent energy to implement those ideas. Is the push first approach sucking intelligent energy away from your implementations?

Putting the Trust = Speed Equation to Work

Understanding produces the one feeling that is most crucial to the success of any organization: the feeling of trust. Here's another statement you can go to the bank with. It's from the book *Values-Based Selling*, by Bill Bachrach and Karen Risch: "People don't trust you because they understand you ... they trust you because you understand them."

Think about it. The people on your "most trusted" list probably understand you. They don't misread your motives or misinterpret your intentions. But it's probably difficult for you to trust someone who misunderstands you. There is an integral relationship between understanding and trust. The deeper the understanding, the more

The deeper the understanding, the more trust is created.

trust is created. Why? Because feeling understood is one of our primal needs. Swiss psychiatrist Paul Tournier puts it this way in his book *To Understand Each Other*: "It is impossible to overemphasize the immense need we have to be really listened to, to be taken seriously, to be understood ... No one can develop freely in this world and find a full life without feeling understood by at least one person."

When someone meets a need that is as primal to us as the need to feel understood, we tend to feel that we can trust that person. And trust is invaluable to productivity. As W. Edward Deming used to say, "Trust = Speed." When trust is in place, decisions can be made quickly and executed without friction. When trust is absent, people sit across the table from you, recognize your idea as a great one, but say, "We better think about it for a while. We're not sure it will work as well as you say." When trust is absent, it can take people days of persuading and fourteen pages of justification just to get permission to buy a photocopier.

Steve's idea was a great one. Had he taken the time to understand his employees' concerns, he could have created trust and trust would have created speed. Luckily, in Steve's case, all that was lost was money, time, and energy. In some situations, like the one below, the cost of push and acquiesce can be fatal.

Big Problem with Push

In January 1986, Roger Boisjoly and Arnie Thompson, two Morton Thiokol (MTI) engineers, strongly and passionately advocated to MTI and NASA management not to launch the *Challenger* space shuttle. They had significant scientific and engineering concerns about the effect that cold temperatures would have on the solid rocket booster seals.

But management would not listen. They marched forward and gave the thumbs up: "It's a beautiful day, go ahead and launch."

Seventy-three seconds into the launch, the *Challenger* was destroyed. An O-ring seal in the right solid rocket booster failed, sending seven crew members to their deaths.

How did this disastrous miscommunication happen?

- Were the leaders operating from deeply ingrained assumptions? "Engineers are always perfectionists – they can't see the big picture. All they can see are the picky little things that *could* go wrong."
- Did time pressures win the day with management? "We've had too many delays already. If we delay again, we'll look incompetent."
- Was management cocky? "Blow-by is not a serious issue. It hasn't burned us before."
- Were political pressures driving their decision? "We can't disappoint the White House or we'll lose funding."
- Was it a "sales decision"? Did MTI fear upsetting NASA and losing out on upcoming rocket contracts?

Whatever their motivations, tragically, management turned a deaf ear to the engineers' objections.

To add insult (and further injury) to injury, despite the sheer magnitude of this tragedy, NASA still did not adopt a Pull approach. NASA managers hit the replay button in 2003, seven years later, in the *Columbia* disaster. Once again, the concern of mid-level engineers – in this case about a possible hole blown in the wing by foam – was squelched. And once again the engineers' concerns were validated. The shuttle blew up upon reentry, and seven crew members were killed.

The final report on this disaster contains this harsh assessment: "NASA's organizational culture had as much to do with this accident as foam did."

Our leaders tend to push and our employees tend to acquiesce.

Wherever you find a strong attitude of push, you will also find the attitude of acquiesce. And that's the grave reality of North American business: our leaders tend to push and our employees tend to acquiesce. The problem with push and equally with acquiesce? Both create costly fatalities. Great ideas get axed before they can be developed. People's commitment and engagement get smothered. Important relationships get broken and destroyed. Ultimately, we fail to uncover the Bigger Reality, which means we forfeit the opportunity to release the intelligent energy that produces smart behaviors and great results.

But, you may argue, isn't there a time to advocate your own perspective? Absolutely. And when is that time? After you have pulled first. When pulling has created a willingness and capacity inside the other person and they are willing to begin pulling from you, you have earned the right to passionately advocate your point of view.

Mental Muscle Memory

A good friend of mine is a police officer. He tells me that the police academy has had to change the way they train their officers, especially in the area of disarming an assailant. In training, an assailant points a gun at an officer and the officer executes a swift technique of grabbing the firearm out of the assailant's hand. Having successfully disarmed the assailant, the officer hands the gun back to the assailant and the cycle is repeated until the technique can be completed flawlessly.

You are probably anticipating where this is going. There is video footage of an officer engaging with a crook in the act of robbery. The crook points the gun at the officer and the officer smoothly extracts the gun from the crook's hand – and then hands the gun back to the crook! I regret to say that the crook then shot the officer.

Mental muscle memory (MMM) is a powerful thing. You walk into your bathroom in the middle of the night and reach for the light switch. Without looking, your hand goes to exactly the right spot on the wall and your finger knows whether to flip the switch up or down to turn the light on. When you drive your car to work, you pass through vast portions of streets and highway without taking in what's occurring. Did I go through a red light? I can't even remember! That's because your drive to work is 90% taken care of by MMM.

The problem with MMM becomes clear when we develop habits

that make us ineffective, where we figuratively hand the gun back. Many of us have such a long history of pushing first in conversation that we have created MMM that is difficult to recalibrate. As if that were not enough of a challenge, there are at least ten other factors that strongly influence us to take a push first approach.

Top Ten Reasons We Push First

1 We operate from a powerful **assumption** that there's not enough time to pull.

2 We feel the need to **judge**.

3 We feel personal **responsibility**. There's so much at stake here I have to push.

4 We cave in to our **ego** and pride.

5 We fall into the **right/wrong trap**.

6 We fall prey to **insecurity** and fear.

7 We lack **modeling**.

8 We don't want to be **perceived as a pushover**.

9 Our culture seems to demand it.

10 We are steeped in **competitiveness**.

Police officer training is different now. After the assailant points the gun and the officer takes it away, he then points the gun at the assailant. That marks the end of the cycle. Officers practice this drill until they have fully recalibrated their MMM. And that's the good news about MMM. Your neural pathways *can* be recalibrated. With practice you can create MMM that will systematically trigger behaviors that are highly productive.

My Own Journey to Pull Conversation

From Listening to Understanding

In 1993, I began working for Eagle's Flight and devoted myself to helping organizations across North America become effective in something that I thought was crucial to business success: listening. I soon realized that although listening was important, it was not the real deal. It was only a mechanism that produced the real deal: understanding.

For the next several years I helped groups of people work through tough issues and achieve understanding. My quest brought me into the world of dialogue.

From Understanding to Dialogue

I delved into the dialogue work of William Isaacs, Peter Senge, and David Bohm. I traveled to the Global Dialogue Institute in Philadelphia to study their approach. I received mentoring from an expert in the field of dialogue, Dr. William Stockton of Mobius, which is an organization dedicated to training business leaders in the art of dialogue.

I garnered the best of what each of these dialogue experts had to offer and began to put their principles to work, helping organizations dialogue through their thorniest issues. I found myself gaining more skill in helping people tackle tough conversations in a way that systematically helped them achieve productive outcomes.

Some people have an innate tendency that can be a blessing and a bane. They *have* to get to the *why* of a concept. I'm like that. I'm impelled to understand the irreducible elements of why something works. Thus I was motivated to find the one underlying principle that each of these schools of dialogue had in common. What one thing made all of them work?

It was the notion of Pull. Pull powerfully attracts clarity to itself. Like a pump or a vacuum, it hungrily draws in understanding. Pull goes far beyond asking questions: it inquires deeply, maintains an undivided focus, strips away ambiguity, and comes back with the trophy – the essence of what the person was really trying to express.

Pull is an attitude that causes you to take such a genuine interest in another person that you actually step out of your world and into theirs. When you execute Pull correctly, you end up seeing and feeling the other person's reality the way they see and feel it.

> *Pull is the humility that hungrily draws out another's truth mixed with the courage to speak your own truth.*

Pull is an attitude that energizes both inquiry and directness. It is a strong desire to understand, mingled with a strong desire to be understood. It is the humility that hungrily draws out another's truth mixed with the courage to speak your own truth. I have come to believe that Pull – this mixture of inquiry and directness – is the one thing that makes dialogue work. And there's a good reason for this.

Dialogue is not just a method of helping people understand each other. It is a way of doing conversation that *gets reality flowing*. It is a radically different form of conversation, and very few organizations or individuals really know how to do it well. We are good at debate and discussion. Unfortunately, these forms of conversation don't produce much reality. Why? Because debate means "to beat down" and discussion means "to shake apart." As popular as these forms of communication are, they are not well suited for uncovering reality. Pull, on the other hand, a mixture of inquiry and directness, has proven to be entirely effective in getting people to reality. Why?

Inquiry can't stop until it discovers what's really going on beneath the surface. *Directness* slices right through pretense and perception. At the heart of both inquiry and directness is a refreshing attitude: "Let's get real."

Dialogue means *reality flowing through*. When we learn how to pull first, we actually begin to draw reality out of each other. We begin to understand and experience each other's reality.

I've had the privilege of seeing powerful breakthroughs occur in the corporate world as leaders in all sorts of organizations did the hard work of going through chaos and coming to a place of transformational dialogue.

But a recurring pattern emerges that short-circuits breakthroughs for some leaders: the dynamic that the people who need to learn dialogue the most feel they need it the least. When they hear the word *dialogue*, it conjures up images of people sitting cross-legged in a circle getting in touch with the ether. They have no use for such an activity. And that became my challenge: how to engage people in a process that they needed but had no use for.

The people who need to learn dialogue the most feel they need it the least.

From Dialogue to Pull Conversation

As I was wrestling with this dilemma, I heard a friend of mine say something intriguing about conversations: *"The quality of your organization is as good as the quality of the conversations of your people."*

That made sense to me. I knew that people's ability to dialogue determined the quality of their organizations. Firsthand experience had shown me that the only way an organization could attain and sustain its best results was to cut through perceptions and conventional wisdom and uncover reality together through dialogue.

But in my quest for dialogue, I had skipped right over the simple notion of conversation. I turned to my dictionary and discovered something very interesting: that conversation means *to turn together*. This notion perfectly captures the essence of what Pull Conversation is all about: two people or groups turning toward each other, using inquiry and directness to pull out each other's reality.

It was at this time, in 2003, that our company, Juice Inc., was conceived, and I began to change my approach, talking to people about Pull Conversations. People who could not relate to the ethereal concept of dialogue easily caught onto this concept. As we went to the business community with Pull Conversation, we began to see some very exciting breakthroughs.

Pulling Out a $1.2-Million Reward

Bill was a manager whose technical abilities were topnotch, but his inability to pull – specifically to inquire into other people's realities – was holding him back from the promotion that he so desperately wanted.

As an engineer in a nuclear power plant, Bill had no choice but to become much better at working with and through others. Unfortunately for him, his lack of empathy and understanding had effectively alienated him from the rest of his colleagues. No one wanted to work with him. And no one wanted to manage him. Bill's career was at a standstill and he was ready to go to the human rights commission because he believed he was being discriminated against.

Bill's organization asked me to be his communication coach.

After meeting him and interviewing some of his colleagues, I knew I was going to be the person Bill hated for a short time but respected for a long time. He was so deep in denial that I knew I would have to be very direct in the way I worked with him. Here's the aggressive curriculum I set up for him:

- Learn the principles of inquiry, especially the skill of pulling out and understanding others' realities.
- Practice that skill in a low-risk situation and receive feedback from me.
- Practice in a medium-risk situation and receive feedback from me.
- Practice in a higher-risk situation and receive feedback from me.

In the first Pull Conversation, Bill did not "get it." I had given him the clear mandate of pulling out and understanding the other person's reality and not giving in to the temptation to justify his behaviors, defend himself, or make himself understood. Time after time I had to halt the process and bring Bill back to his mandate. Time after time he gravitated to pushing.

I gave Bill very candid feedback about his performance. So much so that at one point he looked at me and asked, "Has anyone ever struck you in a coaching session?" Bill appeared to be a very explosive man. Perhaps I had watched too many cop shows, but I remember driving home from those sessions and checking my rearview mirror to see if I was about to be run off the road.

The second conversation was not much better. Bill just couldn't seem to get the concept of Pull. His habit patterns were deeply imprinted with a push-first style of communication. Once again I had to give Bill the very feedback he did not want to hear.

Something happened in the third conversation. Bill exerted significant effort. It felt as if he was starting to turn the corner. At last he was starting pull out the other person's reality and understand where they were coming from.

Over a period of several weeks, Bill kept working on his curriculum. Imagine how juiced I was when I got a call from the human resources supervisor, who said, "You won't believe it, but Bill just saved the company two million dollars!"

I definitely couldn't believe it, so I phoned Bill's direct supervisor and asked him, "Is this true? Did Bill just save the company $2 million?"

"Well, we thought it was going to be $2 million, but it turns out the savings is $1.2 million. The Atomic Energy Commission (AECL) had proposed a course of action that was going to be far more expensive than it needed to be. Bill picked up on the areas of waste."

The supervisor then, in effect, summed up the nature of Pull Conversations. He reported that in the past, Bill would have come in calling people idiots, getting their backs up. The proposal would have been pushed through despite his colleagues' resistance. This time, as the supervisor described it, he pulled out their reality and understood their interests. Then he framed his concerns in ways that they could understand and buy into. He pulled them into his reality, got them on board, and the company was able to move forward with a modified process that saved $1.2 million.

Like David in Chapter 1, Bill achieved significant results by:

- Foregoing his tendency to be defensive and instead pulling out the reality of the AEC team, which created receptiveness in them.
- Pulling them into his reality in a way that they could understand and buy into.
- Uncovering the Bigger Reality, by asking: "What is it we both want here that will allow us to move forward?"

Communicate Less?

So many people have been battered with the injunction, "Communicate more. Communicate more." But we're here to say, *communicate less, but with messages that slide right into the listener's world.*

Every minute you spend pulling out someone's reality enables you the economy of framing your message in a way that appeals to their interests.

The Components of Pull

Pull is a blend of two "heartsets" that work elegantly together to help you get to reality: inquiry and directness.

Inquiry

Inquiry was made popular in the fifth century B.C. by a fellow named Socrates. Inquiry is the drive to deeply understand and be open to another's reality. Inquiry goes far beyond showing an interest. It takes interest a step further, into the new terrain of raw need. "I *need* to know your viewpoint. I *need* to know what's going on inside you. I *need* to find out what you are thinking and feeling." Like a magnet, Pull powerfully attracts clarity to itself. Pull goes far beyond asking questions: it enables undivided focus, strips away ambiguity, and comes back with the trophy – the essence of what the person was really trying to express. And sometimes more.

Inquiry has an openness to it that makes it a close cousin to humility: the teachability that looks for reasons to be impressed by others' ideas rather than to invalidate them. There is a vulnerability to humility – a willingness to be imprinted with someone else's beliefs and feelings.

Directness

Directness is a strong drive to be real and to get to reality as quickly as possible. Directness enables you to straightforwardly assert your reality to others face to face, as opposed to by an indirect approach: sending your message through someone else or through an indirect medium like email. Directness transcends most people's definition of honesty (telling the truth). It takes you to a place of *not withholding* what's going on inside you. Directness means being open to telling your truth and getting it "out there" into the world. Naturally the discernment filter needs to be on. Naturally you need to determine how, when, and what information to share and with whom you should share it.

There's a passion component of directness that makes an imprint on your listener. As you'll see in Chapter 2, it is critical that leaders go beyond facts and learn to share their emotions through the use of stories and symbols. As Jim Rohn, America's business philosopher, says in his keynote speeches, "Effective communication is 20% what you know and 80% how you feel about what you know."

The Pull Matrix

The model below shows how inquiry and directness work together in conversation. If they're both fully present, two people or groups can:

- Uncover the Bigger Reality.
- Reach a shared understanding.
- Create high levels of trust.

The Pull Matrix

Directness	HIGH	**Push**	**Pull**
A strong desire to be understood, marked by frankness, persuasion, authenticity, honesty, candor, reality, advocacy and passion		Little understanding Little trust Little reality	Significant understanding Significant trust Significant reality (Bigger Reality)
		Withdraw No understanding No trust No reality	**Acquiesce** Some understanding Some trust Some reality
	LOW		HIGH

Inquiry
A strong desire to understand, marked by openness, curiosity, humility, seeking, searching, vulnerability, empathy, exploration, and discovery of others' frames of reference

Because conversation means *to turn together*, it makes sense that both inquiry and directness are required. When you inquire directly, it makes the other person feel that they can turn toward you and share their reality with you. Consider:

- *Turning together requires trust and respect.*
- *Trust is largely created through inquiry, and respect is largely created through directness.*

Various types of one-way conversations happen in the quadrants where inquiry and directness are not fully present. The only time a Bigger Reality can emerge, however, is when two people or groups show up with both inquiry and directness and neither is functioning at the expense of the other.

Note that while some may assume that inquiry and directness are mutually exclusive, it is possible to do both at the same time, as the following examples illustrate.

How Inquiry and Directness Work Together

Damian says something offensive in a meeting. Melissa approaches him afterward and says, "Damian, I have concerns about your comment in the meeting, but first I'd like to understand your rationale. Then I'll share my concerns."

Melissa is framing the conversation by being direct. ("I have concerns.") She demonstrates a desire to inquire into Damian's reality. ("But first I'd like to understand your rationale.") Then she lets him know that she's going to be direct about her concerns after she has understood him. ("Then I'll share my concerns.")

Kim loses a family member. When she comes back to work, most people skirt her work area, not knowing what to say. Eric picks a time that he believes will be most appropriate and says, "Kim, may I ask how you are doing? I have no idea how you must be feeling but I'd really like to know if there's anything I can do to help. Would you like to talk?" It takes directness to broach this type of conversation, but Eric does it in way that is fully blended with inquiry.

Jeffrey meets Nicole in a social setting and she expresses a strong desire to have him call on her and do a sales presentation to her group. Jeffrey leaves two emails and three voice mails for Nicole with zero response. He leaves a voice-mail message that says, "Hi, Nicole. I have no desire whatsoever to waste a minute of your time. I left our conversation at the dinner a few weeks ago with a clear understanding that you wanted me to pursue a meeting with you and your group. To be frank, I must admit that I have become frustrated with your lack of response to my emails and voice mails.

I would love to understand if your world has just become too crazy to do this or if something has changed for you that makes this meeting unnecessary. I am completely fine with either a yes or a no, I just don't want to waste either of our time. Let's take five minutes on the phone to determine whether this relationship should move forward or not. You can reach me at (123) 456-7890."

In a meeting that feels like a waste of everyone's time, Juan does a process check and says, "I have to be honest. This is not working for me. Is it just me, or are we off track right now? Does anyone else here feel we're getting stuck?" Once again, a blend of inquiry and directness.

What Are We Really Saying Here?

- You can distinguish yourself from two-thirds of the culture by pulling first rather than pushing first when you have a point to get across.
- The most critical preparatory step in getting people to understand you is creating capacity in them through Pull Conversation.
- Pull Conversation is not just about listening more. Although deep and thorough listening is definitely a component of it, Pull is more than that. It is a very direct, active type of inquiry that slices through assumptions and perceptions because it *has* to get to reality.

Want to Make This Happen?

- Look at yourself through the eyes of your co-workers and your family and plot yourself on the Pull Matrix. What is your growth edge?
- Do you need to develop your inquiry skills to balance out your directness? (See Chapter 3.)
- Do you need to be more direct to balance out your ability to inquire? (See Chapter 4.)

Juice at Home

Cody's Lawn

I was training members of a large manufacturing company in the southern United States in how to reach their goals by understanding one another. Their goals had for some time eluded them, as warring departments bickered, wasted time, and created roadblocks. After I had worked with the company for about two months, Rick, one of the machinists, told me a story of how the training had saved him from blowing it with his son, Cody.

Like many of the other machinists, Rick was skeptical about this dialogue stuff. He was a nuts-and-bolts, give-me-results-*now* kind of guy. He had neither the time nor the stomach for sitting around and yakking.

But strangely, the Pull Conversation concept stuck with him. It followed him home. It kept rumbling around in his head.

One weekend, Cody, Rick's eight-year-old son, cut the lawn by himself for the first time. It was a hot day. Through the window, Rick could see Cody pushing hard, sweat trickling off his chin, the dust and grass flying up around him.

Forty minutes later, Rick heard Cody burst through the door, stop abruptly as he remembered to take off his grassy shoes, then come pelting down the hallway.

"Dad!" he called, "Dad! Come and see. I finished it. Come and see the lawn!"

Cody grabbed Rick by the hand, and Rick grinned at his son's glistening, grimy face.

But as Cody dragged him out to the yard, Rick experienced several emotions at once. All across the lawn, straggly uncut grass marked Cody's wayward path. The lawn was going to have to be done all over again! Rick was annoyed. Didn't Cody know better than this?

Rick was ready to lay into his son for doing such a shoddy job. But just before it was too late, a small thought flashed through his consciousness. It was a story that I had told about stepping into my son's world to pull out his reality, seeing and feeling a situation the way he saw and felt it. Rick's instinct was to push a good piece of his mind on Cody. Instead, to his credit, he turned toward his son and chose to first pull out his reality. He tried his best to step into his son's world, looking at the lawn through an eight-year-old's eyes. What he saw through Cody's eyes was a great job. He also got in touch with Cody's need to feel approved and valued.

"Good job, Cody," he said, giving him a big hug.

There would be plenty of future opportunities to coach Cody on his grass-cutting skills. Rick's split-second insight had transformed this moment into an opportunity for celebration.

Pull Out Their Reality

3

Harnessing the Power of Context

*W*E'VE discovered that Pull Conversation has a logic to it. When you blend inquiry and directness, it fosters feelings of respect and trust in others. This, in turn, calms them and increases their capacity to understand you. Inquiry and directness are perfectly suited to get you to a Bigger Reality, and getting to a Bigger Reality tends to release intelligent energy in your environment. This chapter demonstrates the results that come from pulling out context and highlights inquiry as the attitude that is most instrumental in getting you the context that you need.

Putting Context into Context

Understanding Produces Context

One of the richest rewards of pulling out someone's reality is context: the ability to see as a sensible whole what others see as disconnected parts. Context is a clear picture of the beliefs, values, and emotional needs that motivate another's actions. And context is produced by understanding. When Bill, as related in the previous chapter, pulled out the concerns and goals of the Atomic Energy Commission, he gained an understanding of their reality. This gave him context regarding how his concerns and theirs could be reconciled. He was then able to frame his message in a way that appealed to their interests. Context made him effective.

Context is a critical ingredient of success in every area of life. It informs you in hundreds of ways about what actions and decisions will yield the best result as you deal with people. From throwing someone a surprise party to negotiating a complex business deal, understanding the context of someone's beliefs, values, and emotional needs enables you to accurately anticipate the approach that will work best for them.

When you are able to interpret and anticipate others' behaviors, you will be outfitted with *relational radar*: the ability to detect what's coming at you before it arrives. Relational radar tells you how to be appropriate in any situation. Charles Garfield tells a story, in *Peak Performers*, illustrating how intelligent energy is released through interpreting context accurately. He relates how a member of the New York consulting firm Inferential Focus spun four lines he read in the *Wall Street Journal* into great profits for his firm's clients. According to these four lines, Saudi Arabia was making a major change in the shipping requirements for incoming goods. Their country had decided to reduce the size of the containers by 50% and were moving from inspecting 80% of them to inspecting all of them.

"The consultant suspected fear of terrorism," Garfield writes. "The Saudis were known to respond to fear by stashing their oil money in a safe place – gold. Inferential Focus told its clients to buy gold. Six weeks later, the value of the gold had doubled."

What Is Context?

Context is the environment that surrounds or influences something. Think of a beautiful wall hanging, perhaps a rendition of the Last Supper. There is a specific black thread that makes up the pupil of Peter's eye. The white and beige threads adjacent to the black thread are the environment that surround and influence it. The different components are woven together and make up the eye and, in a global sense, the whole picture.

This is a particularly apt analogy, because context literally means to weave together (*com* = together; *texere* = to weave).

In the story above, the lines in the newspaper were like four strands of thread. The Inferential Focus employee looked beyond the four strands of information to the Saudi environment that surrounded them. As he looked at the surrounding strands of information, he saw the fear of terrorism woven together with the tendency to stash oil money in a safe place. These surrounding strands became the context that made the first four strands of information make sense and spark a smart strategy.

The analogy of weaving may be applied in another sense. Having or not having context into someone's behaviors is like the difference between looking at the back or the front of a tapestry. From the back, each of the threads looks random and senseless. But step around to the front of the tapestry and the threads on the back make sense.

The Inferential Focus consultant looked at one side of the Saudi behaviors – the change they were making to their shipping requirements – and instead of dismissing these behaviors as random or senseless, sought to pull out the Saudi reality, seeing their behavior through Saudi eyes. As he did so, he saw and felt the threat of terrorism. This peek at the front side of the tapestry made sense of the "random behaviors" on the back.

Then the consultant went one step further. He pulled out the implications of the behaviors. He asked himself, if they are afraid of terrorism, where will they stash their money? Historically, the answer was "gold." This view from the front of the tapestry made the smartest decision become clearly apparent: "Tell our clients to buy gold." The outcome of the story confirms the rewards of seeking out context: more output with less strain.

Let's think of our dealings with people. On the surface, we see their actions. As we try to make sense of what those actions mean, we typically believe that we are looking beneath the surface to understand the motives behind those actions. But because motives are invisible, we tend to turn to the only form of meaning-making we know, assigning our own motives to the other person's actions. The logic chain goes something like this:

> I'd have to be feeling really angry to say what Sylvain just said to me. He must be really angry with me. I wonder what motivated him to be so angry. I must have said or done something to tick him off.

There is one problem with assuming that others have the same motives we do. Given how different we are, the chance that we're right is very slim. Here's where pulling out the other's reality serves us. Pulling out an understanding of Sylvain's reality gives you context. For instance, perhaps you discover that he is very comfortable with being direct and speaks his truth forcefully just to get it off his chest. He isn't even close to anger yet. This context enables you to interpret his words and actions more accurately.

Would those who know you best characterize you as someone who takes the time to pull out their reality – to understand the context behind their behaviors?

Drowning in Info, Starving for Context

I've heard it said that thirty years ago, the primary role of the manager was to give employees enough information. Today it's different: employees are drowning in information but starving for context. Employees receive hundreds of emails every week packed with information. What they lack is the ability to understand what much of the info means to them in their role.

You can provide real value to your employees here. I know a great manager who has this figured out. As he puts it, "I tell my boss, 'Send all your emails to me and I'll relay them to our employees. Some of them I will send through as they are. Others I will write a short introduction to explaining the context of how this information is relevant to them. Some of the emails I will filter out, making the call that they don't need to know that right now.'"

Truly Understanding

Pulling out someone's reality is another way of saying *understanding someone*. The problem with the word *understanding* is that, like many of the words we use, it has been trivialized and plundered of much of its richness. In our business, we have enabled many people to become more effective at conversation by offering them a richer definition of the word. The definition comes from stories about neighbors.

A Tale of Two Neighbors

I know of two neighbors in my home town who had a bit of an altercation a few winters ago.

Yanek is a helpful sort of guy who likes to use his snowblower to blow out his neighbors' driveways and sidewalks. Yanek was especially glad that he could help Carl and Joanne, who had recently suffered the loss of their baby girl.

The day after blowing out Carl's driveway, Yanek met him out on the street. To his great surprise, Carl walked over to him and told him in vividly clear terms never to blow out his driveway again. Carl would shovel the driveway out himself.

Yanek could not understand Carl's irrational reaction. He complained to my friend Sean, "Why would a guy get so angry and react like that when all I wanted to do was help him out? I understand he's grieving, but can't he accept a little help?"

As Sean showed Yanek the other side of the tapestry, Carl's "irrational" behavior made a lot more sense.

"Carl and Joanne's baby died because she overheated," Sean told him. "They brought her in from the vehicle and left her in her baby seat because she was sleeping. By the time they checked on her a little while later, she had died. Carl told me the only way he can get relief from his grief is by doing something physical. Shoveling snow is his only outlet.

"When you blow out his driveway, you leave nothing for him to do. He's got no way to work things out."

This instantly made sense to Yanek. The moment he began to see and feel Carl's reality, he understood Carl's response.

> *To understand is to see and feel someone's reality.*

This is the beginning to a helpful definition of the word *understanding*. To understand is to see and feel someone's reality.

Seeing and Feeling

When we use the word *see* in this book, we mean emotional as well as cognitive seeing. It's not enough to understand someone intellectually. People want and need to be understood empathetically. Throughout this book, when you read the phrase *to see someone's reality,* read it as *to see and feel someone's reality the way they see and feel it.*

Understanding someone in this way does not mean you agree with them. It does not mean you would feel the same way in that situation. But if you can demonstrate that you see their reality, chances are they will feel understood by you, whether you agree with them or not.

Now let's look at a metaphor that will fill out this definition.

A Tale of the Roses

Imagine that you have a neighbor, Maria, who is a rose fanatic. Her life revolves around roses. She talks about roses, thinks about roses, and spends all her time, money, and energy on roses.

Now, you're not against flowers. Like many people, you have a few flowerbeds. But inwardly you believe that Maria is a little over the top with her rose obsession.

One day you are having a conversation with her over the hedge and Maria is gushing about how beautiful her roses are. Not wanting to get drawn into a lengthy account of the latest flower show, you shut the conversation down and walk away, wondering to yourself, "What *is* it about these roses that captivate her so?"

A while later you are looking out your kitchen window. You can see the back side of a few roses as you peer through Maria's hedge. "What's so special about those roses?" you ponder.

Because you are interested in getting better at pulling out other people's realities, you decide it's time to find out why Maria loves roses so much. You step out of your home and make the trek to Maria's door. As you knock on her door, you wonder what you may be getting yourself into.

Once you are seated and into your conversation, you say, "Maria, I know you are passionate about roses and I've never taken the time to ask why. But I'd really like to know. Why do you love them so much?"

"There are several reasons, but let me show you the main one," Maria says.

She leads you to her kitchen and throws open the window, which overlooks the most amazing rose garden you have ever seen. The sights and the smells of the roses hit you with equal force. Maria begins to tell you about her earliest memories, of helping her mother in her rose garden back in Yugoslavia. The fondest memories of Maria's life derive from those lush moments with her mother in that garden.

Then Maria tells you something deeper behind her memories. Recently her mother was killed in the ethnic battles of her country. Maria's rose garden not only reminds her of good times with her mother, it is a memorial to her memory, and it helps her deal with her grief.

Now that you see and feel Maria's reality the way she sees it and her rose obsession makes sense to you, you face a choicepoint: do you reflect your newfound understanding back to Maria, or do you simply let her finish telling her story and walk out of her house?

The most appropriate behavior is to reflect back to Maria what you have understood her to say.

"Now I know why you love roses so much. I am deeply touched by your love for your mother and how you are honoring her. Thank you for sharing this experience with me."

Maria is honored that you spent the time to hear her story. Meanwhile, your views about how she spends her time and what she talks about have undergone a massive shift as a result of your newfound understanding.

What did it take to gain this understanding? You had to take several actions:

- Exit your house.
- Walk down your driveway.
- Walk on the sidewalk toward Maria's house.
- Walk up her driveway.
- Climb her steps.
- Knock on her door.
- Ask if you could come in.
- Walk into her house.

But if you had to reduce all those actions into two main actions, what would they be? The first action you had to take to see and feel Maria's reality was to *step out of your world*. The second was to *step into her world*. When you step into Maria's world, it is relatively easy to see her reality the way she sees it and to reflect back to her what you have seen.

This now fills out our definition of understanding. To understand is *to step into another's world, see their reality, and reflect back what you have seen.*

These are the three elements that are outlined under Step 1, "Pull Out Their Reality," of our Pull Conversation Model.

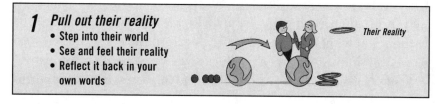

1 Step into Their World

Helping thousands of people acquire this skill has convinced me that you cannot step into someone else's world until you first leave your own.

Is leaving your own world easy to do? For most of us, it is brutally difficult. My world feels secure. It's all that's comfortable and safe for me. The thought of stepping outside my world produces fear inside me.

Kofman and Senge explore this fear in their essay "Communities of Commitment: The Heart of Learning Organizations." According to them, true learning of *any* kind feels dangerous, because learning occurs between a fear and a need. On the one hand, we feel the need to change if we are to accomplish our goals. On the other hand, we feel the anxiety of facing the unknown and unfamiliar. To learn significant things, we must suspend basic notions about our worlds and our selves. That is one of the most frightening propositions for the ego.

Stepping into the Customer's World I

Fred deVries (his real name) made the sale of a lifetime a couple of years ago. As a medical equipment sales rep, he was trying to land a deal with a large Ontario hospital. As it turns out, it's a good thing he got the sale. Having invested a year of his career, hundreds of hours of time, and many thousands of company dollars in doing so, it would have been a tragedy to have emerged empty-handed.

Since this was the largest sale in the history of the company, Fred was flown down to Texas to share his secrets with the North American sales reps. Rather than playing the guru, Fred brought someone from the hospital to give her account of why he got the sale. Here's what she told the reps:

"Get to know your customer. Fred spent as much time as possible with us. He got to know each of our little wins, what scratched our itch, how often each of us wanted to see him. He invested in us without knowing if he would get the deal. In the end it was clear to us we weren't just buying a product – we were buying a company."

Fred stepped into his customer's world at every possible opportunity. Here's how:

- He made it his business to understand what a "little win" was for each decision-maker. This enabled him to make the most of his time and energy investments.
- He maintained a detailed profile sheet on all of the key players. This kept him from making assumptions.
- He spent time with the nurses where they worked. This enabled him to clearly understand the aspects of his company's instruments that were most valuable to them.
- He sponsored nurses' trade shows and anesthesia research software. This demonstrated his support for them and their profession.

- He wrote down, remembered, and referred to the tiny "wouldn't it be nice requests" of the people he called on. This clearly demonstrated that he understood what was important to them, what made them light up.
- He invited doctors on trips to view the equipment. This demonstrated his understanding of their need to manage risk.

In the final analysis, Fred's ability to step into his customer's world catalyzed trust and yielded him the most dynamic result of his career: a $7.8-million sale and an $11.5-million year – which was 403% of his quota. More output with less strain.

2 See and Feel Their Reality

Technically speaking, it is probably not possible to *totally* leave your world and *totally* step into someone else's. Stepping into another's world is more about making their frame of reference (how they see the world) your *primary focus* and your own frame of reference your *secondary focus*. If a surgeon is excising a malignant piece of tissue from your body, her primary focus is the damaged tissue, and her secondary focus is the way the scalpel feels in her hand. If she decides to shift her focus and concentrate on how the scalpel feels in her hand, she will quickly find herself botching the surgery by cutting too deeply or removing too much or too little tissue.

If you have been focusing on your own "stuff" (concerns, interests, need to be right, assumptions, and judgments), you may be finding that you're not effective at stepping into other people's worlds. And it's quite possible that you've been botching some important conversations as a result. Perhaps people are walking away from you more wounded than healed. Now is the time to begin a new habit of stepping into other people's worlds and making their stuff your primary focus. This is the most effective way to see their reality, and it is the most effective way to gain a clear sense of context into their words and behaviors.

This is not the common practice. I have asked participants all over North America, "How many of you had parents or teachers who taught you how to step into someone else's world and see their reality?" Fewer than 10% respond that they had been taught to do this well. Perhaps you feel the same way. The good news is that it's not too late to learn this crucial life skill – and that doing so can make a difference not only in your professional life but in the lives of the people closest to you. The following story gives a practical example of how to step out of your world and into someone else's and what can occur for you when you do.

I'm Not Taking Music!

A decade ago my son Adrian was in grade nine. He was taking music in school and was doing well in learning to play the trumpet.

One day we were driving down the road together and he said, "I'm dropping out of music next year."

My inner emotional response indicated that I was hearing this statement from inside my own world. I wanted to default to push-first behavior, to say, "Adrian, people would kill to be able to express themselves on an instrument like you do and you're going to just throw it all away?"

I didn't say that. Instead, I thought to myself, "I *teach* people how to deal with these situations. What am I supposed to do here?"

Attempting to step into Adrian's world and pull out his reality, I asked, "You want to drop out of music? Can you tell me about it?"

"Well, I have to write all these essays on Beethoven and Chopin. They don't help me improve as a musician. I just want to spend my time getting better on the trumpet."

I was almost tempted to dash back into my own world and say, "But the cultural appreciation these essays will give you for music is so critical, Adrian..." It took a great effort for me to inquire about what was going on in his world, because doing so required me to step out of my own world and leave behind:

- My assumptions: "He just lacks perseverance."
- My judgments: "If he can't persevere, he'll never amount to anything."
- My fears: "If I try to understand him, he might perceive that I'm condoning this bad decision. What if he ends up being someone who caves in when the going gets tough? I'll look like a failure as a dad."

Somehow, I stepped into a fourteen-year-old boy's world and saw his reality. When I felt his desire to play the instrument and get hot on doing the riffs, writing the essays felt like sludge. I reflected this back to Adrian.

"These essays sound really boring," I said.

"They *are* boring, Dad. But I won't want to stay out of music forever. And if I go back in grade eleven, I'll be in with a bunch of grade nines because the class is a nine/ten split."

Again I stepped into Adrian's world to see his reality. "Being in grade eleven and having to go back in with the grade nines and tens sounds like it would be kind of awkward," I said.

Within a few minutes, we pulled into our driveway. Adrian turned to me and said, "I'm taking music next year."

I wondered to myself, "I didn't coerce him, argue with him, or persuade him. So what was *that* all about?"

Today, I know exactly what it was about. Did Adrian perhaps have an inkling of what my position would be regarding his dropping out of music (especially considering that I am a musician myself)? Of course he did. He didn't really need me to give him my views on the importance of sticking with the music program.

He *did*, however, need to feel deeply understood by his dad. As I stepped out of my world and into his, he felt understood by me. He *knew* deep inside that I felt the boredom and drudgery of having to write essays when you want to play your instrument. He felt no judgment or disapproval, only understanding. And remember Paul Tournier's salient words about understanding quoted earlier: "No one can develop freely in this world and find a full life without feeling understood by at least one person."

Understanding is one of the best ways I know of drawing someone's brilliance out. Because Adrian did not have to exert one brain cell outmaneuvering me or out-arguing me, he could put all his mental energy into making a great decision. His decision-making capacities were escalating to the place where he could consider the consequences of both decisions and make a great choice.

Once in a while you get it right. In this situation I was fortunate enough to be able to show support and understanding in the midst of my son's complicated decision. In the years that followed, Adrian's musical interests and abilities mushroomed. Today, he is talented musician, expertly playing many instruments, writing and recording his own music, and producing CDs professionally in his own studio.

Let's break down exactly what happened:

- Stepping out of my own world meant leaving my assumptions, judgments, and fears behind.
- Stepping into Adrian's world meant inquiring into his thoughts and feelings without judgment or coercion. ("Tell me about it.")
- Seeing his reality meant picturing in my mind's eye what he was going through.
- Reflecting it back meant being willing to give him back his feelings in my words. ("That sounds boring.")

If I had not stepped out of my world and into Adrian's, I would have breached trust with someone I love very much.

His subsequent track record has proven that my assumptions, judgments, and fears were unfounded. Adrian does not give up easily and he knows how to stick with something until he masters it.

Let me ask you a question: Whose world do you need to step into? What assumptions, judgments, or fears do you need to leave behind in order to step out of your world? Doing this successfully requires a powerful and reliable source of energy. The best energy source I know for enabling you to discover someone's reality is the attitude of *Pull.* Let's turn our attention to that powerful attitude now.

Pull Is the Learner's Path

I've heard it said that half of what we learn in life we learn by the time we are five years old. I'm not sure if that is true, but I do know that a child's ability to master new concepts and acquire new skills is breathtaking.

The Sales Expert

Molly approaches everything with an attitude of Pull. She has a learner's heart that expresses itself with inquiry, openness, and humble curiosity. In her first year, little Molly will learn how to negotiate a bottle, crawl, and walk. By the end of her second year, she will have a working knowledge of the structure of one or two languages. In her third year, the attitude of Pull will begin to show up in her language: "Why, Mommy?" "What's that, Daddy?" From age three to four she will pull out every discovery she can and begin to master numbers, shapes, colors, even learning some social skills. Every time she experiences a new breakthrough, she will feel a sense of gratification. You know what it feels like. You feel it when you master a new aspect of PowerPoint or discover a better way of chipping shots onto the green.

For Molly, life is about the joy of experiencing new things, and learning is the fun path that gets her there. Her Learner's Path is expansive and meandering. It has hundreds of offshoots and bunny-trails. She defaults to this path because it is fun and she has learned that going down this path yields delicious, rewarding experiences.

For the first five years of Molly's life, she is perpetually pulling, and she does it in a very direct way. The rewarding experiences at the end of the Learner's Path and the fun nature of the path itself energize her in her quest to learn. Almost every question produces a rewarding experience: an exciting new piece of knowledge about a color, a skill, a letter, a word, a shape, or an animal.

Molly is now five years old and she has fixed her gaze on a PlayStation. It seems that she won't rest until she gets one. Remember what your kids were like when they wanted something? Now think about Molly's sales approach, asking the questions W. Timothy Gallwey outlines in his book *The Inner Game of Work*:

- Does she develop rapport with the buyer?
- Does she handle objections creatively?
- Does she know the buyer's hot buttons?
- Is she direct?
- Does she ever fail to ask for the close?
- Does she customize her sales approach to each buyer?
- Does she fear rejection?
- Is she resilient? Optimistic?

Molly has learned to do naturally what sales VPs spend hundreds of thousands of dollars trying to drill into their sales forces. How did she learn her selling skills? Pull. Pull energizes Molly to closely observe and pay focused attention to the *buying behaviors* (not the selling behaviors) of her parents. As she observed them, she made subtle adjustments in her approach until she found a systematic way to get to the rewarding experience she was seeking.

Losing the Path

Then Molly gets sent off to school. Traditionally, what do our educational systems reward kids for? Questions or answers? Inquiry or certainty? You know the answer! Molly begins to learn that it is the answer that makes her successful, not the question. She begins to go down the Learner's Path not because it is fun or because it will give her a rewarding experience but because at the end of the path she will find answers. Answers that will buy her the marks she needs from her teachers. Answers that will buy her the affirmation she needs from her parents. Answers that will buy her the social acceptance she needs from her peers. The Learner's Path is no longer playful, meandering, and filled with endless side trails. It is the short, straight, perfunctory path of commerce.

By the time she exits the educational system and plunks herself into her first job, she will learn that a person of *certainty* is much more valued than a person of *inquiry*. People who ask questions are annoying. They make people bristle. They waste time in meetings. People roll their eyes at them. Molly begins to steer away from her innate tendency to inquire. As she does so, her penchant for directness begins to fall by the wayside as well.

Ultimately, the Learner's Path inside Molly becomes virtually closed off. By the time she is fifty-five, *certainty* will have set in so solidly that she will barely remember how to learn – or to pull. She has ceased to be a learner and is now a judger.

The most effective leaders are the ones with the right questions.

Learner Questions versus Judger Questions

The most effective leaders are not the ones with the right answers but the ones with the right questions. When you ask a well-crafted question, it's like pulling back a bow inside the mind of your listener. It produces creative tension. In the milliseconds that follow, the person's mind is racing, sifting, sorting – trying to lay hands on the arrow that will hit the mark and answer your question. This creative tension has the capacity to produce deeper thought and change in a person than your answers ever could. That's because, as Marilee Goldberg Adams says, "Questions predictably cause new openings for action, whereas statements and opinions rarely do."

But there are questions that lead to great outcomes and there are questions that lead to not-so-great outcomes. How do you know which are which? The same writer has coined language to describe

Examples of Learner and Judger Questions

Learner Questions	Judger Questions
"What do you think is possible here?"	"How do you expect us to finish this on time?"
"Are there other avenues we should explore?"	"Where's the money going to come from to pay for this?"
"What can we learn from this?"	"Why did you let this happen?"
"Where are you getting stuck?"	"Can't you see what you're doing wrong?"

The judger is filled with certainty and feels no need to learn. This attitude oozes out of each of the judger questions above in the form of a certainty-filled statement:

- *"This can't be finished on time."*
- *"There isn't enough money for this."*
- *"You could have prevented this."*
- *"You must be blind. It's obvious to me what you're doing wrong."*

These questions are not driven by inquiry – they are driven by interrogation. Unfortunately, inquiry, teachability, openness, and humility are sadly missing in the judger. Ask yourself this: Would the people who know you best characterize you as more of a learner or more of a judger?

two types of questions: Learner Questions and Judger Questions. "Learners ask genuine questions, which are those to which they don't already know the answers," Adams writes. "Learner questions typically presuppose fresh possibilities, a positive future, and abundant resources." Judger questions "lead to automatic reactions, limitations, and negativity and they focus attention on problems rather than solutions."

"Holy Curiosity"

"The important thing is not to stop questioning. Curiosity has its own reason for existing. One cannot help but be in awe when he contemplates the mysteries of eternity, of life, of the marvelous structure of reality. It is enough if one tries merely to comprehend a little of this mystery every day. Never lose a holy curiosity."

— ALBERT EINSTEIN

The Learner's Heart

There is a humility associated with Pull that expresses itself in directness, openness, and vulnerability. Directness is an attitude of undisguised straightforwardness. Openness is an attitude of teachability that looks for reasons to be impressed by another's comments rather than to invalidate or compete with them. Vulnerability is an attitude of willingness to be imprinted with someone else's beliefs and feelings without feeling the need to be defensive or guarded.

It's easy to see why adopting the attitude of inquiry is so critical to your ability to step out of your own world and into someone else's. It takes a lot of humility, directness, openness, and vulnerability to leave your assumptions, judgments, and fears behind and step into someone else's world seeing their reality the way they see it.

Similar to the blend of inquiry and directness required to master Pull Conversation, humility and professional will are now finally being recognized as the crucial components of successful leaders, thanks to author Jim Collins and his research team. Collins documents this in *Good to Great*, a book about how some companies go from being good to being great, and some don't.

The genesis of his book is an excellent example of the Learner's

Path and where it can take a person. It seems that Bill Meehan of McKinsey and Company commented to Collins at dinner one night that his previous book, *Built to Last*, was "useless." Instead of shutting Meehan down or laughing off his comment, Collins was curious and asked him to explain what he meant.

"The companies you wrote about were, for the most part, always great," Meehan said. "What about the vast majority of companies that wake up partway through life and realize they're good, but not great?"

Collins, being a man of Pull, opened himself up and made himself vulnerable to that simple remark. And the reward of inquiry was great. As Collins puts it, "Meehan's comment proved to be an invaluable gift, as it planted the seed of a question that became the basis of this entire book."

Collins avoided falling into the trap of hubris, the swollen ego that believes, "There's nothing I can learn from you." Hubris spawns a certainty that is the enemy of inquiry. Certainty doesn't allow for that *more*. It doesn't allow for change in others. The truth is that each of us is always learning and changing, so there will always be more to discover. Hubris doesn't allow for the complexity of each individual.

Humility, the antithesis of hubris, is the natural state of children. They have little pretense or sophistication. For instance, they thrill to the experience of learning the new skill of dressing themselves and are oblivious to the fact that their underwear is on backwards and inside-out.

The good news is that humility – adopting a learner's heart – is a choice. You can choose to humble yourself and ask a question when something is ambiguous. You can choose to humble yourself and inquire deeply into someone's reasoning. Every time you humble yourself and ask, the Learner's Path within you becomes more and more expansive. Soon the thought of going down that path will begin to energize you. You will find yourself wanting to learn a new language, pick up a musical instrument, or learn how to optimize the use of your PDA.

One of the best ways to develop your capacity for inquiry is to learn the art of respect. Respect is the engine of inquiry. When you truly respect someone, it is much easier to want to understand what they are thinking and to inquire into their world.

The great news is that respect is a choice. It is not a special attitude that only certain people are equipped with.

As you'll discover in Chapter 6, respect literally means "to look again." Instead of hearing someone's words and discounting them as worthless, you can choose to look again for their true potential, to look again for value that you may have missed at first glance. Respect will energize you to inquire more deeply and you will begin to experience richer relationships.

More Output/Less Strain

So far we've said that Pull is the attitude that energizes you to see another's reality. If you do that well, the prize you get is context: the ability to perceive as a sensible whole what others see as disconnected parts.

Before you step into someone's world, you fully own your perspective, but very little of the other person's. After you step into their world and see and feel their reality, you own two perspectives: yours *and* theirs. Context about their world broadens and deepens your perspective. This makes you more effective as a decision-maker, a problem-solver, an innovator, a negotiator, and a people-developer.

> The smartest decisions and actions become apparent to the person who steps into another's world.

Mark it well, the smartest decisions and actions become apparent to the person who steps into another's world. As the following story illustrates, this produces a lovely combination of more output with less strain.

Stepping into the Customer's World II

Rob LeBlanc is achieving significant sales success and getting lots of "lay downs," much to the envy of his peers at the car dealership where he works. There's nothing sweeter than a customer walking into a car dealership to hand over the full sales price of the vehicle. Getting to the place where your customers trust you enough to give you lay downs is the dream of every car salesperson. Why does this happen to Rob so often? Because he has discovered the secret that stepping into his customers' worlds and seeing their reality is the quickest way to get this kind of result.

"It wasn't always that way," says Rob. "I was way too uptight when I started off. I would meet the customer and immediately go into my 'blurb' – the hundred hot things I thought they should know about the car. I ended up saying things that were not valuable to them and wondered why they balked when I went for the close. In many cases I think I was confusing or frustrating them out of the sale. I lost some deals and elongated others. Worse yet, price turned into the biggest decision-making factor – just the thing you don't want."

Rob faced a crucial choicepoint early in his career. There was one particular salesman who was achieving the highest volume of sales in the dealership by using very forceful sales techniques. He used badgering, guilt, and strong-arm persuasion to get people to buy. Would Rob pattern himself after this sales guy in order to get quick results? Fortunately, Rob saw through him as a person who got the numbers but never got any repeat customers.

Rob had a hunch that repeat customers were the key to long-range success. He decided to use exactly the opposite approach with his customers. His approach would be:

- Easygoing.
- Low pressure.
- Respectful.
- Understanding of customers' specific needs.
- Helpful in showing customers how he could meet those needs.

Rob began to learn that simple questions unlocked the sales process. He started to ask, "What's important to you in a car? What did you like about your last vehicle?"

Every question pulled out responses that helped Rob step into his customer's world. Soon he was understanding their reality: their specific definition of value of performance, looks, safety, maintenance, or theft protection.

This allowed Rob to do three things:

- Point the customer to exactly the right vehicle.
- Highlight only the benefits that mattered.
- Do so in the language that would create a quick and lasting impact.

Next, Rob would invest time in a leisurely test drive, further highlighting the benefits that were important to the customer.

"Now, you said that performance was important for you. Why don't you put your foot down on the gas pedal and see what this thing will do off the line?"

Or, "You were asking about protection for your kids. If your little girl was back here where I'm sitting and the vehicle was hit from the side, here's exactly how the side air bags would provide maximum safety for her."

By the time the test drive with Rob is done, the customers feel that he has deeply understood their reality. The net result for Rob? By spending this kind of time up front, he spends very little time in the price negotiation phase.

Many people, feeling pressure to get results quickly, jump right to making decisions and taking action without investing enough time in drawing out data and understanding reality. Rob, and many of the clients we have worked with, have found that the quickest way to get to sustainable results is to invest the time to understand reality. When you do, it becomes apparent what course of action will yield the best results.

Stepping into Your Product's World

Designers and marketers have discovered that you can even step into the world of the product or service that you are bringing to your customers. Michael Michalko gives a fascinating example in his book *Thinkertoys*. As Michalko tells it, the CEO of a small company that sold wall coverings had an odd way of thinking about his product and market. He constantly asked himself, "What would wall coverings say to me if they could talk?" It got to the point that he began to think he *was* a wall covering.

Fear of fire was one answer he came up with given the coverings were made of highly toxic materials. Noting that the conglomerates made such coverings, the CEO of the small company developed its own nontoxic, fire-resistant fiberglass material. This company then sent flyers to distributors, architects, and others who choose or buy wall coverings. The flyers detailed the high toxicity of the giants' vinyl and polypropylene wall coverings and emphasized the danger of litigation. In the event of fire, the victims or their estate could file a class action suit naming the property owner, the architect or engineer who specified the dangerous wall covering, the distributor, and the maker liable.

The result? The public abandoned the big manufacturers and made the CEO and his small company a great success.

When the CEO stepped into his wall coverings' world, he was really stepping into his customers' worlds. This doubled his perspective and made him more successful as an innovator and problem-solver. Once again – more output with less strain.

Top Ten Obstacles to Stepping into Other People's Worlds

1 No perceived benefit.

2 No time or energy.

3 No skills or experience.

4 "Insurmountable history" and past issues.

5 Fear of being rejected or ignored.

6 Defensiveness, pride, and the fear of having to admit you're wrong.

7 Fear of being perceived as agreeing with the other's viewpoint.

8 Preformed assumptions and judgments.

9 Fear of being perceived as weak or subservient.

10 Faulty beliefs (such as "understanding = agreement").

The most crucial thing you need to do to step into another's world is to be real.

Be Real

The most crucial thing you need to do to step into another's world is to be real. Remember, *who you are works*. Who you wish you were or who you are trying to be like doesn't work at all. Do not try to step into another's world synthetically (for example, asking questions to pretend you're interested). People will sniff that plastic and exclude you from their world fast. They will withhold their best stuff from you and you will end up devoid of the context that fills their words and behaviors with meaning.

Understanding Your Self

Get Past Your Self

As Narcissus admired himself in a pool, he became enamored of his own image. Leaning in to kiss himself, the handsome young man drowned, swallowed up by his own image. Self-absorption brings death. It's a tragic tale and it can happen to any of us.

Although Narcissus sounds like a fool, it is quite possible that this has happened to you from time to time. It certainly has to me, and whenever I get swallowed up, it's my self-image that sucks me in. In some conversations, I can't step into other people's worlds because I'm too deep into my*self* and can't seem to get out. See if any of these "self" issues keeps you from stepping into other people's worlds:

- **Self**-absorption swallows up your ability to be thoughtful and consider others' interests.
- **Self**-consciousness swallows up your ability to be observant of others' subtle verbal and nonverbal expressions.
- **Self**-righteousness swallows up your ability to admit you are wrong and others are right.
- **Self**-ishness and self-love (narcissism) swallow up your ability to see and care about others' needs.
- **Self**-doubt, fear, and insecurity swallow up your ability to venture out of your place of safety to explore others' beliefs, judgments, and feelings.
- **Self**-defense and justification swallow up your ability to listen to others' concerns and take ownership of your behaviors.
- **Self**-pity swallows up your ability to empathize with others.

It is essential to become aware of these diseased behaviors as you engage in conversation.

Taking Stock

Thankfully, not all self is diseased. There is perfectly healthy self-esteem, self-love, and self-respect. If you want to find out if a particular behavior is healthy or diseased, here's a good rule to follow. Ask a few of the most honest, trustworthy people you know, "When I _____, do you feel it produces positive results in me and in those around me?"

Be prepared to step into their world as they give you their answer. Your mission is to see yourself as they see you. Don't defend yourself, justify yourself, or feel sorry for yourself. If trusted people tell you that your "self" behaviors are not producing positive results, it's time to make some changes.

This is a chance for you to take stock. Where are you with respect to getting over your self and learning to step into others' worlds? Below are some diagnostic statements. Picture the person who knows you best filling this out. Write down, from 1 to 5, what you believe their responses would be about you. (1 = *strongly disagree*; 5 = *strongly agree*)

- This person frequently asks questions and inquires about what's going on in my life.
- When I'm speaking, this person seems genuinely interested in what I'm saying.
- This person comments on the subtle things that go on in our conversations.
- The way this person inquires into my needs leaves me feeling that they are authentic and genuine.
- Rather than defending their own beliefs and judgments, this person explores my beliefs and judgments.
- This person seems more interested in understanding me than in being right.
- When confronted with their behaviors, this person begins by seeking to understand my point of view versus justifying their behavior.
- Rather than seeking sympathy, this person is primarily

focused on expressing their concern for what others are going through.

3 Reflect It Back in Your Own Words

The power of the mind's eye is an undervalued life skill. Being able to visualize something in its completed state enables effective problem-solving, contingency planning, and visioning.

Excellent builders can look at a blueprint and see in their mind's eye the three-dimensional building taking shape. This enables them to anticipate exactly what labor and material will be required at each stage, never being caught unawares.

A good leader can observe team interactions and visualize in her mind's eye what the human dynamics will look like in a given set of circumstances. Seeing the human "architecture" play itself out in a merger or acquisition situation enables her to anticipate and avoid needless human friction. Good leaders use this skill to maximize the output of their employees with less strain.

A talented performer foresees herself in front of her audience and pictures in her mind's eye a stellar performance taking place. When it's time to perform, she has already been there, executing every move flawlessly. She simply has to follow along.

Stepping into another's world is really about perspective-taking: seeing another's point of view and getting inside their frame of reference. Imagination, or the mind's eye, is the faculty designed to enable you to do these things effectively. Our definition of understanding says it well: understanding is stepping into someone's world to see their reality the way they see it. You can't see someone else's reality without the faculty of the mind's eye.

When you are in conversation, begin to picture in your mind's eye what the person is speaking about. Imagine what it's like to be them in that situation. For example, when my son Adrian was talking about the essays he had to write, I could picture the boredom of that scene. This enabled me to reflect back his reality accurately, so that he felt completely understood.

Pull Conversation is one of the best ways to develop the capacity of your mind's eye.

Picturing What You Haven't Experienced

Picturing someone's reality is more challenging when they are describing something to you that lies outside your experience. But it is still possible.

Let's say that a colleague feels that a comment that you made in front of the leadership team has hurt his reputation. He has just stepped into your office to take you to task for this. You want to step into his world to see and feel his reality the way he does. However, you yourself have never felt this way in front of the leadership team. What can you do?

- Identify the speaker's basic feeling. (Betrayal)
- Go to your bank of experiences and locate one that is related. (Your best friend in high school led your teachers to believe that you had been cheating on your tests.)
- Get in touch with the feelings that surrounded that experience. (Blinding anger, knot in the stomach, inability to sleep.)
- With those feelings as your starting point, use the power of your mind's eye to imagine what this person is feeling and to picture him in the situation that he is describing to you.
- Finally, reflect back your best guess of what the person is feeling. ("I imagine you're feeling like you've been stabbed in the back?")

Note that stepping into this person's world does not mean that you are agreeing with them or admitting that you have wronged them. What it does mean is that you are helping them feel understood rather than spending your energy justifying your words and actions. It is the St. Francis of Assisi principle: seeking first to understand, then to be understood.

Also note that you are imagining what it's like to be them in the midst of their situation. You are picturing your friend in his situation rather than picturing yourself in his situation. The one thing that is problematic about putting yourself in another person's shoes is that it's still *you* that's in their shoes. Putting you, with all your values, beliefs, motivations, likes, and dislikes, in that person's shoes doesn't really give you an accurate understanding of their reality.

Gaining empathy through experience (walking in someone else's shoes) is great, but just make sure that you use that understanding to step into *their* world and see *their* reality the way *they* see it. In a 1959 essay, Carl Rogers defines empathy as the ability to "perceive the internal frame of reference with accuracy, and with the emotional components and meanings ... as if one were the other person but without ever losing the 'as if' condition."

"I Know What You're Feeling"
Remember, people don't need (and often don't want) your autobiographical account of what it's like for you to be them.

Empathic Listening

Empathy is the ability to feel what someone is feeling without their having to tell you. Empathy, in fact, means "passion in." Listening empathically is the process of getting someone else's feelings in you, then reflecting them back.

Every "stream of conversation" is really two streams. There's the information stream, bearing the topical content. And there's the meaning stream, a deeper stream containing values, beliefs, and feelings. Anyone can pull out the surface content, the words of anger or frustration. Only empathic listeners can pick up on the deeper emotions under the surface. And once this deeper context is understood, it gives meaning to every word in the flow of information.

Here's an example of someone who does a good job of pulling out not only the surface stream, but the meaning stream beneath it.

Jeff and Todd have been working on a project together and they are about to go into a meeting with their boss, Jerry. He has a reputation of ripping people apart psychologically if he senses that they are not on top of their stuff. Before going into the meeting, Jeff and Todd agree that each of them will step up to the plate to answer questions within their domain of expertise.

Shortly after they enter Jerry's office, he starts to ask Jeff some pointed questions about why some recent time lines have not been met. Jeff pauses, waiting for Todd to jump in – this is obviously his area of expertise. But Todd doesn't say a word. This ignites Jerry's anger. He begins going after Jeff, asking rapid-fire questions, beginning to call his knowledge, and then his competency, into question. Finally Jerry says, "What am I paying you for, Jeff? Get out of my office and get your act together."

Jerry and Todd slink out of the room and go to their own offices. Two minutes later, Jeff comes storming into Todd's office, growling, "You owe me an apology, you %&*@!"

"You are *ticked*," Todd says.

"You're ^%#&* right I'm ticked. You'd be mad, too, if that happened to you."

"I guess you felt totally discredited in there?"

"Of course I did. You made me look like an idiot in front of Jerry! You and I had an agreement."

"You feel I betrayed you, don't you?"

"What else could I be thinking?"

"Well, as tough as it is to feel embarrassed and backstabbed, I bet what was really going through your mind was, 'How am I going to take care of my family if Jerry fires me?'"

"You've got it. That's exactly what I was thinking. What was going on in there, Todd? How come you left me hanging out to dry?"

"Jeff, I don't know what happened. My mind went totally blank. I saw what was happening to you and I was mortified, but I was like the deer caught in the headlights. I'm really sorry."

Todd made a good call not to get defensive or try to apologize at the beginning without knowing the full extent of the damage he has caused. Instead, he stepped into Jeff's world, felt his reality, and reflected it back, going one stream deeper each time. Anybody can reflect back, "You're ticked." It takes more skill to pull out and reflect back:

- "You felt discredited."
- "You felt betrayed."
- "You were afraid of being fired and losing your livelihood."

Pull Conversation will require you and enable you to stretch

> *Pull Conversation will require you and enable you to stretch beyond the rudiments of active listening.*

beyond the rudiments of active listening. By stepping into the other person's world and feeling what they feel, you'll be able to do what we call the "implication reflection": reflecting back not only the person's feeling but the implications of what that feeling means to them in their world.

For example, Todd not only reflected back Jeff's feelings of embarrassment, he also stepped into Jeff's world to feel the implications of that feeling: "I'm going to lose my livelihood here." Reflecting back the implications makes the other person feel deeply understood and produces feelings of rapport and trust.

How to Listen Empathically

Use your ears to capture the info stream and your eyes and "gut" to detect the emotions from the meaning stream. People's nonverbals are the most reliable tip-off to their feelings. The body tends to tell the truth. Watch:

- Their eyes.
- Their hands.
- Their posture.

These will typically broadcast the truth. It is easy for a person to delete or distort with their words, but it's difficult for them to do so with their body.

Once you feel their feelings, you need to reflect them back. To be effective at reflecting back their feelings, you need three basic components, preferably framed in your own words.

1 *A tentative statement*: "It sounds like ..."
2 *The essence of the feeling*: "... you're angry ..."
3 *The situation that caused the feeling*: "... because I forgot to call."

Here are some examples of this:

- "It seems as if you feel left out because you don't have Calvin Klein jeans like Molly and Jody."
- "It sounds as if you're feeling overloaded by my expectations."

- "I hope I'm following. You're suspicious about Anne's motives?"
- "Do you feel angry about not being consulted?"

How Deep Do You Go?

Reflect surface feelings first, then try to feel and reflect underlying feelings. Here are two approaches to take:
- **First, go as deep as the situation warrants.**
- **Second, go as deep as your partner feels comfortable going.**

What Are We Really Saying Here?

- Context is Queen. It makes the smartest decisions and actions become apparent.
- The way to get context is to step into the other person's world and experience their reality.
- This skill (experiencing another's reality) is more instrumental than any other in making you successful in every area of your life.
- To step into someone's world, you have to be able to step out of your own.
- To do that you have to shift from self-centeredness to other-centeredness.
- Re-engage yourself in the activities that require you to have a learner's heart.
- Exercising Pull Conversation will develop the capacity of your mind's eye.
- Go beyond active listening and reflect back not only the feeling but also the implications of that feeling.

Want to Make This Happen?

- What relationship do you most need to be working on right now?
- This relationship will be your practice ground for the Want to Make this Happen? sections of this and the next two chapters.

- Do all the prep work on a copy of the Pull Conversation Model before booking your conversation with this individual.
- Start out by writing out your assumptions about the individual and the situation. What will you need to do to step out of your world and step into theirs?
- What areas of your world do you need to be willing to temporarily leave behind?
- What learner questions will you ask to enable you to see and feel their reality?

Juice at Home

"I Don't Want to Go to School"

The best moms and dads step into their kids' worlds so they can understand their concerns, fears, needs, and goals. Seeing and feeling your child's reality the way they do enables you to be effective in coaching them to make great decisions.

I used the skill of stepping into my daughter Katelyn's world to help her through a long phase of not wanting to go to school. Many nights I would go into her room to say good night and she would say, "I don't want to go to school!"

Inside *my* world I was thinking, "Oh you're going to school all right. There's zero budge-factor on this one." But instead of dragging her into my world, I stepped into hers. Using a skill from Adele Faber and Elaine Mazlish, in their book *How to Talk So Kids Will Listen and Listen So Kids Will Talk*, I walked through these simple steps:

- I listened attentively to her complaints about school without giving my rebuttals.
- As I listened, I acknowledged her comments and feelings with short responses: "Hmmm," "I see," "Oh."
- Next, I gave the feelings a name. "That must be annoying."
- Next, I gave Katelyn her wishes in fantasy. "I wish you didn't have to go to school either! I wish you and I could

fly to Disneyland for cotton candy and then go to Switzerland for a toboggan ride and then go to Italy for an ice-cream cone. I wish we could just have fun all day long. What do you think about that?"

- Finally, I would empathize by saying, "I wish we could go to Disneyland together, but I have to go to work and you have to go to school. I know it's hard when something so important like going to school is so tough to do."

I'm thankful to say that walking through this process never failed to transport Katelyn to a place of feeling that going to school was once again bearable. But to do this, I had to resist the temptation to drag her into my world and tell her, "You're going to school. That's the end of it!" As I look back on that phase, I realize that Katelyn was clearly aware she had to go to school, all she really wanted was to have her feelings accepted and understood.

Pull Them into Your Reality

Tapping the Power of Pull

*I*N the previous chapter we concentrated on the first step in Pull Conversation, the skill of pulling out the reality of other people. Now we're going to explore the second step, pulling others into your reality. We have discovered that when two people *see* and *feel* each other's realities, astonishing *changes* can take place.

Harvard change expert John Kotter describes this phenomenon in his book *The Heart of Change*. He tells of how he used to believe that what people needed was analysis. Analysis would make them think differently and thinking differently would make them change. After years of experience, however, Kotter learned that the reliable sequence was not *analyze, think, change* – it was *see, feel, change*. People see something compelling and they feel a powerful feeling in their gut. That feeling moves them to a place of embracing change.

Kotter tells a great story of a large manufacturing organization in which purchasing had clearly gotten out of hand. Individual plants all insisted on doing their own purchasing and the waste in the system was hemorrhaging company profits, to the tune of $200 million a year.

As a head-office leader, Jon Stegner had a summer student working for him and he decided to conduct an experiment. He had her go to every plant and bring back every type of glove they purchased and mark the price paid for each pair. After the student had collected the gloves from all the different plants, he had her pile all 424 pairs on the boardroom table. Then he invited the division presidents into the boardroom, all of whom promptly began circling the table and its pile of gloves.

As Kotter puts it, "They looked at two gloves that seemed exactly alike, yet one was marked $3.22 and the other $10.55. It's a rare event when these people don't have anything to say. But this day, they just stood with their mouths gaping."

The glove demonstration went on a traveling road show to every division and dozens of plants. "The road show reinforced at every level of the organization a sense of 'this is how bad it is.' "

As a result, a mandate for change ensued that saved the organization a very great deal of money.

> *Human beings are not changed by information. They are changed by interactions with other people.*

Human beings are not changed by information. They are changed by interactions with other people. Here's where we begin to see some of the transformational potential of Pull Conversation. When done well, it enables people to embrace change more quickly than perhaps anything else can. So let's focus on what you can do to Pull others into your reality where they can *see and feel* what's important to you. The core elements of this skill are illustrated in Step 2, "Pull Them into Your Reality," of the Pull Conversation Model and are covered in detail in the rest of this chapter.

2 Pull them into your reality
- Invite them into your world
- Help them see your reality
- Ask them to reflect back what they've understood

Your Reality

1 Invite Them into Your World

There are two ways to invite someone into your world. The first is to simply ask them to listen to you. When you know you've stepped into someone's world, seen their reality, and reflected it back to their satisfaction and they still aren't showing any signs of trying to understand you, it's time to be direct and make your needs known in a straightforward way: "I think I understand your point of view now. May I ask you to listen to mine?"

When you do this, people will sometimes say, "I think I understand where you're coming from." Then they will give you their take on your point of view. One of the following things may happen as a result:

- They may have understood your point of view precisely and you just weren't aware of it. Now you know they've got it.
- They may have understood most of your point of view but are still unclear on a few aspects. Now you have a chance to clarify their understanding.
- They may have entirely misunderstood your point of view. Now you have a chance to correct a misunderstanding or missed understanding.

Whatever happens, you have moved both of you closer to uncovering the Bigger Reality. This gets you closer to unlocking productive results in your situation.

The second way to invite someone into your world is to use language that lives for them – language that intrigues them and is easy for them to relate to and understand.

Use Language That Lives

Stories, metaphors, analogies, and illustrations are effective means of inviting a person into your world. These communication tools not only create a curiosity in the mind and heart of your listener, they also make a lasting imprint. You know this. Think of the databytes that have riveted themselves to your memory. They probably came to you framed in "story."

It is good to be reminded of this story dynamic; otherwise we are in danger of slipping into a one-dimensional communication style: all facts, and no emotions or symbols.

Consider what Boyd Clarke says on this point, in *The Leader's Voice*: "When your intent is to move people to action, to help them understand and deepen their appreciation and gain more insight and more passion about their work, you have got to have all three [media]: facts, emotion, and symbols."

Clarke calls symbols "shorthand ways of conveying both emotion and meaning." He adds that although facts are vital, they lack meaning and impact until we blend them with emotions and symbols.

As Theodore Kinni writes in the *Harvard Business Review* of May 2003, "Relying on facts alone, despite their power, is a doomed strategy. When a leader communicates via only one channel, the receiver is forced to make sense of the information by filling in the blanks on his own – and the meaning that the receiver creates is often not what the communicator intended."

Clarke says that "adding the other two channels in the appropriate ways at the appropriate times dramatically increases the chance of the communication getting through."

Sing to the Goose

What a paradox: the more power and authority you have, the harder it is to get your hands on reality.

I've discovered that CEOs rarely get the whole truth told to them, or if they do, it's so sanitized and so carefully couched that the reality rarely gets through. What a paradox: the more power and authority you have, the harder it is to get your hands on reality.

As a consultant/coach, my business will live or die by my ability to pull leaders into my reality by speaking my truth productively. I remember sitting with Frank, a CEO whose organization was deteriorating. His stores were underperforming and his employees felt exploited. They had bought the dream and had made him wealthy. But he was demanding more and more without showing any appreciation for their contribution. Frank had recently lost it in a leadership meeting, raising his voice and lowering his credibility with many of his leaders.

I had interviewed every person at head office, determined to discover what needed to occur to stop the deterioration of the company and get Frank's business back on track.

I spent a good amount of time listening to Frank, making sure that I completely understood his reality. I could tell his capacity to understand my point of view was growing. Now my job was to tell a story that would pull Frank inside my world and enable him to see my reality. You'll recognize the story I told him as a takeoff on one of Aesop's well-known fables:

> Once there was a king who was given a goose with an unusual talent. The giver of the goose said, "If you sing to this goose, she will make you very rich."
>
> Every day the king would come and sing to the goose, and when he did, the goose would lay a golden egg. Although the king was becoming very wealthy, he grew impatient for more. He thought to himself, "If my singing causes the goose to lay one golden egg, think how many she will lay if I yell at her."
>
> So he went to the goose and yelled at her, "Lay more eggs, you useless goose!"
>
> To his utter amazement, the goose laid five eggs over the next two days. But then she stopped laying altogether.
>
> "Hmm. I know what I must do," thought the king. "I will threaten the goose. Perhaps that will cause her to lay many eggs at once." He went to the goose, laid his hand on her neck, and said, "Lay eggs or I will wring your neck!"
>
> This approach produced a wonderful outcome. The goose laid three eggs in one day. But then she stopped laying altogether. The king decided to take desperate measures. "I will cut the goose open and get all the eggs at once." As he did this, he discovered there was nothing inside her. He stood there in horror, realizing that he had now destroyed his means of creating wealth.

I said to the CEO, "Frank, as you are probably already aware, your people represent the goose that lays the golden eggs. You used to sing to them, but somewhere along the road you started to yell at them, believing it would boost their productivity. It did – but for a short time only. Now you have your hand on their necks and you are threatening them. Frank, you are about to kill the goose that lays the golden eggs."

Frank looked at me and said, "What are you asking me to do?"

"I believe you need to have a conversation with each of the leaders you yelled at in that meeting and apologize to them," I said.

Frank took immediate action. He did apologize to them and began to sing to the goose again by listening to his people and recognizing their contributions. Frank had been pulled into my world by the power of an invitational story. Within the story, he was able to see and feel something that produced a change in him.

I checked in with one of Frank's executives in the following months and was happy to hear that there had been a significant breakthrough in the results of his stores, caused, in large part, by a dramatic rise in company morale.

Stories Are a Springboard

Stephen Denning, author of *The Springboard*, worked in the World Bank and was charged with the task of implementing a knowledge-management solution that would serve the organization's employees around the globe. In theory, this on-line repository of acquired wisdom had great appeal. In practice, it was a monumental task that was made next to impossible by the stalwart stubbornness of change-resistant decision-makers throughout the bank.

Denning amassed a persuasive set of statistics and studies and embedded them in an impressive PowerPoint presentation. He met with constituents of the bank globally, walking group after group through his ironclad, impassioned appeal for a knowledge-management system that would give World Bank employees the information they needed in a matter of moments, no matter what continent they were on. The response was always the same. "It looks like an interesting idea, but we don't think it will work here."

Then Denning heard a story that gripped his attention. It was an account of a Zambian health-care worker who was trying to treat a case of malaria. The worker got onto a computer in the middle of nowhere – Zambia – and logged onto the website of the Centers for Disease Control in Atlanta, Georgia. In moments, the worker was able to procure the exact information required to successfully treat and save the patient's life.

Denning had a thought: "What If I simply told people the story of the Zambian health-care worker? What would their response be?"

In his next meeting, he told the story and watched as the group responded.

"Hey, imagine if we could do something like that," one participant said. "Our employees could log on and get the information they needed to serve our customers. It wouldn't matter where they were or what time zone they were in. Why couldn't we implement something like this?"

Denning was stunned. This simple story created more of an impact in two minutes than all his statistics, studies, and PowerPoint presentations had in two hours. When people saw themselves inside this story, they were able to *see and feel* the implications of having data accessible to everyone in the organization everywhere. This produced a change inside them and they were able to embrace Denning's recommendation of a web-based knowledge repository.

Denning went on to tell the story across the World Bank and it won the day, transforming staunch resistors into impassioned champions of the process he was recommending.

2 Help Them See Your Reality

After you have invited the other person into your world, it's time to help them see your reality. There are two ways to do this: the first is to be direct, the second is to speak your truth productively.

Be Direct

Directness has two meanings: straightforwardness and immediacy. I'll deal with the immediacy aspect of directness first.

Immediacy has to do with going face to face whenever possible rather than resorting to less-direct forms of communication like phone or email. Face-to-face conversation is the conduit that conveys

Face-to-face conversation conveys the greatest amount of emotion, trust, and understanding. the greatest amount of emotion, trust, and understanding between people. I'm thankful for email and voice mail and I think they have made us more efficient and effective. But I also recognize their limitations for handling the robust flow of inner resources that need to be shared between human beings. A big part of being effective as a communicator is knowing the best medium for specific messages. Do you think we may be turning to email too often and to send the wrong types of messages?

Research would suggest so. A global study of the phenomenon was published by communication experts at Rogen in the July– August 2004 issue of *International Association of Business Communicators*. In it they report that more than 80% of their respondents "prefer to receive good or bad news and other important information face-to-face." They go on to say:

> In focus group discussions supporting this study, employees told us of frustrating incidents where leaders had communicated vision statements, performance reviews and even sackings first by e-mail. Two thirds of executives surveyed said that if a major initiative in their organization was delivered first by e-mail, it was not generally more persuasive than if it were delivered face-to-face.

Some of you may be thinking, "Oh great, I work in a virtual team – what am I supposed to do with this face-to-face stuff?" I'll address this for you very soon. First let's see why face to face works best.

Why Face-to-Face Conversation Releases Energy

Just like the feeling of electricity on Dino's primary-belt crew, as described in Chapter 1, energy can jump from one person to another very quickly if the right conditions are present. More often than not, face-to-face conversation is the activity that creates those conditions. There are three reasons why.

- The first has to do with what scientists call the *emotional contagion* caused by the "open loop" in our brain circuitry.

- The second has to do with *trust-building hormones* that are released in this type of conversation.
- The third has to do with our ability to quickly "click" with each other when our eyes pick up on the speaker's *nonverbal cues.*

If you want to release intelligent energy in your workplace, it's important for you to know the basics of how these three dynamics work.

Emotional Contagion

You never have to be concerned about your blood getting mixed with someone else's just because you're sitting beside them. That's because your circulatory system is a closed-loop system. In contrast, the limbic system of your brain (the emotional center) is an open-loop system. That means emotions can be contagious. Someone's tears or their smile can trigger an involuntary sympathetic reaction in you.

In their book *Primal Leadership*, Goleman, Boyatzis, and McKee discuss this open-loop phenomenon and describe how emotions spread between people. They cite studies in which scientists measure the heart rate of two people as they have a good conversation. At the beginning of the conversation, their bodies are functioning at different rhythms, but fifteen minutes later "their physiological profiles look remarkably similar – a phenomenon called *mirroring*."

> Scientists describe [the limbic loop] as "interpersonal limbic regulation," whereby one person transmits signals that can alter hormone levels, cardiovascular function, sleep rhythms, and even immune function inside the body of another ... The open-loop design of the limbic system means that other people can change our very physiology – and so our emotions.

Put us together in face-to-face conversations and we regulate each other's emotions. You've probably experienced this yourself. One team member's strong, buoyant mood affects one person after another until the whole team is feeling upbeat. Another member's critical, negative mood can equally infect an entire team in destructive ways. These authors go on to say:

> This circuitry also attunes our own biology to the dominant range of feelings of the person we are with, so that our emotional states tend to converge. One term scientists use for this neural attunement is *limbic resonance*, "a symphony of mutual exchange and internal adaptation" whereby two people harmonize their emotional state.

When you need to convey optimism, passion, purpose, or seriousness, your best bet is to do it face to face.

In short, when you need to convey optimism, passion, purpose, or seriousness, your best bet is to do it face to face. As a leader, you send out a wavelength that everyone starts resonating to. You can use this open-loop phenomenon to powerfully serve your entire organization.

Trust-Building Hormones

When trust needs to be built, use face-to-face conversation rather than defaulting to the other media. Why? First, face-to-face conversation increases trust, bonding, attention, and pleasure. Secondly, it reduces fear and worry. As Halowell puts it in his *Harvard Business Review* article:

> Nature ... equips us with hormones that promote trust and bonding: oxytocin and vasopressin. Most abundant in nursing mothers, these hormones are always present to some degree in all of us, but they rise when we feel empathy for another person – in particular when we are meeting with someone face to face. It has been shown that these bonding hormones are at suppressed levels when people are physically separate.

That explains why it's easier to rip someone apart in an email than it would be if you were face to face with them. But face-to-face conversation not only produces trust, it can be the happy Prozac moment of your day. Hallowell adds that "scientists hypothesize that in-person contact stimulates two important neurotransmitters: dopamine, which enhances attention and pleasure, and serotonin, which reduces fear and worry."

Nonverbal Cues Are Meaning-Makers

Researchers long ago discovered that when people sense ambiguity between your verbal content and your nonverbal content, they will place the weight of their trust on the nonverbal content to provide the clarification they seek. Face-to-face conversation gives you the luxury of blending your nonverbal with your verbal content. This gives your hearers the richest and most reliable blend of meaning-making you can offer them and allows them to "click" with you more quickly in conversation. When your nonverbals cannot be experienced by them, they turn to their assumptions to supply the context they are missing. And, as we'll see in Chapter 5, their assumptions can be the most dangerous interpreters when it comes to translating your meaning.

Don't put yourself at the mercy of people's assumptions. Choose direct, face-to-face conversation as often as time and geography will allow. This is the quickest way to produce understanding. However, having said that, I need to debunk a destructive communication fallacy that you may have been laboring under.

Perhaps you've run into the 7%–38%–55% rule. A trainer tells you that *"research has shown"* that people extract 7% of their meaning from your actual words, 38% from your tone of voice, and 55% from your body language. If this was true, it would mean that a walloping 93% of your message is communicated through nonverbals.

There are two problems with this rule. First, it doesn't make sense. Second, it comes from a small piece of research intended to demonstrate one particular point and is now being misapplied, becoming a sweeping generalization of how interpersonal communication works.

The research was conducted with college students in the 1960s by a UCLA professor named Albert Mehrabian. It has been very interesting to research his research. If you are curious, you can find a summary of his findings in the Appendix to this book.

Words are very important. You and I both know that you can read a letter from someone and walk away with a very high level of understanding, despite the fact that you have no clue about the tone of their voice or their nonverbals. And if you sit across the table from your boss and say those 7% words, "I intend to have your job within six months," your 93% open body language, charming smile, and syrupy tone of voice will not sway him to feel completely unthreatened by your statement.

In short, amplify the clarity of your message by utilizing face-to-face conversation, but never fail to appreciate the importance of your words for carrying the weight of your meaning.

Pull Conversation for a Virtual World

Email has taken a bum rap. Yes, it has probably been overused: we all chuckle at the commonplace stories of an employee spending five minutes composing an email to a co-worker in the next cubicle, who then takes two minutes to read it and three minutes to compose a response. Ten minutes is expended in reading and writing where a two-minute conversation could have neatly done the trick. And yes, while it is trickier to convey emotional content through email, it is possible – you can find articles and workshops devoted to the topic.

Here are a few simple guidelines to help you use Pull Conversation to release intelligent energy through email.

1 First, before composing an email, step into the other person's world and ask yourself the question, "Is this the best way to send this message or would face to face or voice to voice be more effective for this person?"

2 Now that you have stepped into their world, think of the language that will most appeal to them. Are they technical or nontechnical, formal or informal, expressive or succinct? Frame your message in the language that will make it easy for them to read and relate to.

3 Although straightforward language is typically best for email, it is important to tone down the level of directness that you use. Directive comments that are acceptable face to face come across as too pushy though email. For example, it feels natural when face to face to say, "You get the draft over to me by 4 P.M. tomorrow and I'll add my part and send it off." Read that comment in the context of an email and it could come across as brash. Using email it would be more appropriate to write, "If you can get the draft to me by 4 P.M. tomorrow, I'll add my part and send it off."

4 If you can't go face to face or voice to voice but need to address emotional content in your message, pull the receiver into your world by giving them a glimpse of your body language. For example, if you are expressing your disappointment about a decision that has been made, you could write, "I'm really concerned about how this will impact my team (she wrote, rubbing her temples)." It only takes a few seconds to embed nonverbal descriptors into your text messages and doing so gives the receiver a visual image that enhances their understanding of the nature and depth of your emotions. Another shorthand way of doing this is to use emoticons to add nonverbal meaning to your text messages. E.g., :)

5 When you read something ambiguous in an email, instead of trying to go any further with the email string, pick up the phone and ask clarifying questions. If it's impossible for you to go voice to voice, then send an email asking for clarification: "I wanted to check with you on your email earlier today. Your comment on me being like 'a dog with a bone' could be interpreted as either admiring my perseverance or being annoyed at my stubbornness. I wanted to make sure I understood your intent. Can you say more?"

6 When, as a virtual team, you do have a chance to meet face to face, focus most of your time and energy on relationship-building rather than the execution of technical projects. Building a strong conduit of trust and understanding while you are face to face will give you the context you need to more accurately interpret one another's cyberspace messages.

Be Direct: Earn Respect

Being direct doesn't always create a warm, fuzzy feeling inside people, but it does create respect, clarity, and sustained results.

Brian was a junior employee, fresh out of college, apprenticing in the trades department, when his boss suffered a heart attack.

The company came to Brian and asked him to take over maintenance. The decision was not an easy one; Brian needed a few weeks to think it over.

He knew that if he accepted the assignment he'd have to make major changes that would be fiercely resisted. Several of the guys in maintenance had been there for twenty to thirty years and traditions were deeply rooted within the department.

The lack of preventative maintenance had created a reactive culture resulting in untimely breakdowns, undue stress, disappointed customers, and excessive overtime. In fact, to meet production's needs, maintenance employees were required to work every Saturday and several Sundays each year.

Brian told the company that he would take the position on one condition: he had to be given authority. He knew his men would go around him to his boss. When they did, Brian wanted to know that his boss would send them back to him. His boss agreed.

Brian prepared for the meeting with his men, many of them several years his senior. He knew he would have to pull his men into his reality very directly and assertively if he was going to implement the significant changes that had to be made. He would still be completely polite and courteous, but there had to be no question about his resolve.

"The day I took over I had a mutiny on my hands," Brian recalled in a discussion with me. "After meeting with my men, the ringleader went around me to my boss. True to his word, my boss sent the guy back to me. I talked to the men and said, 'You know how it's been around here? I'm telling you today that it will never be the same. You're working sixty-five to seventy-two hours a week, including Saturdays and Sundays, and you end up paying so much tax on all the overtime that you're not really coming ahead. Not only that, but either this plant or the London plant is going to be shut down. If we don't prove this plant can be viable, you guys won't have a job to come to. If that happens, you'll lose all the weeks of vacation time you've saved up. We're going to become a team of professionals instead of putting out fires all the time.'"

Brian immediately initiated changes to the layout of the plant, roles and responsibilities of the workers, and the processes and systems. The reaction of the men was immediate and violent. One day Brian found himself cornered by three big men. They threatened that if he did not back down he would be taken out back and beaten.

"I knew that was a critical moment. If I backed down here I would lose all my credibility. I held my ground, once again walking them through how my changes were going to make their lives better. I didn't know if they were buying what I was saying, but they never beat me up."

In the months and years that followed, Brian's credibility grew and he won the respect and loyalty of his employees man by man. The few who still covertly tried to sabotage his methods, Brian met with one-on-one, persistently speaking his truth to them. Today, thirteen years later, Brian is experiencing the following results:

- He has a committed, loyal, high-functioning team that supports his initiatives.
- His plant is not only still operating, it was voted as having the most progressive maintenance team in the family of companies. (The London plant has closed down.)
- In the first year, his team worked only four Saturdays and no Sundays (to the delight of management and, in time, his employees).
- In the first year, his changes garnered the company more than $200,000 in savings.
- His team implemented a highly effective preventative maintenance process that virtually removed the reactivity from the system.
- They also implemented a new boiler system that is saving the company $150,000 per year.

Brian's story gives us a few pointers on how to be direct in a productive way.

- Borrow the style that will be most understandable to the people you are relating to. It was crucial that Brian approach his men with a very gutsy, no-nonsense message and back it up with aggressive action.

- Frame your message in a way that appeals to the interests of your hearers. Brian appealed to his men's desire to keep their jobs, keep their accrued vacation time, and compete with the London plant.
- Be consistent. Brian's persistence over time was every bit as important as the initial force of his message.

Why We're Not Direct

There are many reasons why people are not direct. Here are the four main ones:

- The fear of having your feelings hurt.
- The fear of hurting the other person's feelings.
- The fear of damaging the relationship.
- The fear of retaliation.

Each of these fears is energized by a lie that we have accepted as truth. A person I know who doesn't speak his truth because of his fear of being hurt got to that point because every time he had an important conversation with his dad when he was growing up, his viewpoint was disapproved of, judged, and put down. He came to the conclusion that, "If I speak up, I will get hurt."

For me, personally, when I don't speak my truth it's because I fear I'll hurt the other person. It causes me angst to make someone feel uncomfortable or embarrassed. I grew up believing the lie that "conflict is bad – it hurts people."

Life assumptions like these ones drive our behaviors in unproductive ways.

It is beyond the scope of this book to show you how to get your assumptions recalibrated. However, your job is to get to the reality that reveals, "I do not have to give in to these fears." That is not to say that these things will never happen to you. It *is* to say that you do not have to *fear* them.

Pay Now or Pay (More) Later

Sharon managed a group of eleven customer service representatives. Brenda, one of the senior CSRs, had worked in the department for thirty-six years. The customers loved her because she was dedicated and technically competent. Her co-workers, however, had no use for her because she was caustic with them. She was abrupt and manipulative, exploding unpredictably and without cause.

Pretty well everyone on the team had asked Sharon to deal with Brenda, but she couldn't seem to bring herself to do it. Sharon knew that Brenda was very sensitive to receiving critical feedback. Historically, trying to hold her accountable had created outbursts of tears and anger. Sharon couldn't bear the thought of hurting her like that. Instead, she counseled the rest of the team to overlook Brenda's foibles and have empathy for her weaknesses. Her justification to herself was, "I'm sure she'll retire within the next five or six years."

By avoiding the work of pulling Brenda into her reality, Sharon had successfully escaped having to pay the cost of being direct with her. The problem is, she was paying a much higher cost in other areas:

- She had lost three excellent employees in the last two years. All three of them cited Brenda as the main reason for their exit.
- The rest of the team was losing respect for Sharon. When she tried to hold them accountable, they shrugged off her comments.
- Teamwork and collaboration were almost nonexistent.
- The CSRs routinely continued chatting to each other while the phone was ringing. Customer service ratings were falling.
- Sharon's stress level was very high and she had begun to dread coming into work.
- Sharon's boss was seriously considering replacing her.

Ironically, even though Sharon would not speak of her disappointment directly to Brenda, it ended up oozing out of her anyway. Brenda felt a silent undercurrent of disapproval coming from her, even when she was smiling and trying to ignore the issue at hand. Sharon was being indirect, holding back her truth and dodging reality. She did so at her own (and others') peril. Living in

Living in unreality causes a silent, invisible seepage of negative energy that destroys results.

unreality causes a silent, invisible seepage of negative energy that destroys results.

Fortunately for everyone, Sharon undertook a training intervention with her team, in which they were equipped to inquire into one another's realities and be direct with one another in a respectful way. Sharon learned to speak her truth. "I can be brutally honest and people react positively," she told me. "People are sharing what needs to be done to build good relationships. Employees are coming to conclusions and solving issues on their own. People are talking and resolving."

Sharon's directness had a positive effect on Brenda and the entire team. They were able to see and feel Sharon's reality and this became the impetus for positive change.

What Indirect Communication Looks Like

My daughter, Rachel, called from high school and wanted me to pick her up from wrestling. Cael, a reliable young lad we know well, had offered to give her a ride home from these classes, but week after week she refused. "I don't want to impose," she always said. Now, once again, she was calling me away from my work.

I began to wrap up some final details but thought to myself, "Maybe I don't need to rush out this very minute. If I'm a few minutes late, maybe Rachel will get the message that she can't commandeer my time at the last moment."

As I drove up in front of the school, I gave Rachel a reserved, "Hello." As we drove along, I acted aloof, hoping my silence would drive my point home: "Next time, don't think you can just refuse a ride and then expect me to come running at your beck and call."

Upon reflection a day or so later, I thought, "That was probably the most ineffective, cruel form of communication I have ever administered. How could I expect she would understand clearly what I was trying to convey?"

I was practicing indirect communication, a toxic form of conversation that actually creates communication cancer. There is one element conspicuously missing from indirect communication: *courage*. It takes courage to pull someone into your reality and tell them directly that you feel hurt, disappointed, or angry. If you have no courage, you will probably resort to using nonverbal messages, disapproving attitudes, critical humor, or public teasing to get your messages across instead of having a direct, face-to-face conversation with them. After all, it takes far less courage to come to a meeting twenty minutes late than to tell the person who scheduled it that you prefer not to have early morning meetings.

> ### Ouch!
> Another form of indirect communication that people use is what I call eStabbing: sending out a scathing email and bcc'ing those to whom you wish to leak juicy information. Or sending an email to request someone's assistance and cc'ing your supervisor so the person is forced to comply.

Being direct and confronting people directly is difficult, but investing in up-front discomfort is far less expensive than the eventual costs of suspicion, broken trust, and lack of collaboration.

As I have watched people carefully over the years, I have made the discovery that indirect communication devours courage.

Character Assassination

> Indirect communication devours courage.

When someone does something that hurts you, you have a choice. You can go to them directly and tell them how you feel or go behind their back and tell someone else how you feel.

When you choose the "no courage required" choice, a bit of courage shrivels up within you. Being a character assassin takes zero courage. If you make this behavior your practice, you will end up with almost no capacity to confront courageously. The prospect of candidly asserting your truth face to face to someone will make you recoil inside.

Conversely, the more you insist on having radically honest, face-to-face conversations and refuse to get suckered into indirect communication, the more courage will grow within you.

Most People Prefer You to Be Direct

I often present an exercise in which participants pair up and practice understanding each other's realities, especially on the topic of how they would like to be confronted. In this exercise, one person asks the other, "If I were to confront you about something that was bothering me, how would you like me to do it?" Then they give the person a list of possibilities:

- "Would you like me to confront you right away or let a bit of time go by?"
- "Would you want me to display emotion or be more rational?"
- "Would you want to be in your office or mine?"
- "Would you want to be in a restaurant or at work?"
- "Would you want me to be direct or take a more indirect approach?"

Although the participants' answers vary on almost every question, there is one question that they are virtually unanimous on: the directness question. Ninety-five percent of any group will typically say that they prefer a direct approach. When I ask them why, they give these responses:

- "I don't like it when people sugarcoat things. They are essentially saying I can't handle the straight truth."
- "Sometimes people couch their words so carefully that by the time they're done I don't know what they've really said."
- "I like knowing where somebody stands. If they are direct with me, I know I never have to worry about them talking behind my back."

If you were to videotape all these people as they confront others, I believe you would discover that only a small percentage of them are direct in the way they do so. The point is, even though only a small percentage of people have what it takes to be direct with you, a large percentage of them want you to be direct with them. When you are direct with people in a respectful way, it increases their trust in you, makes you more credible in their eyes, and causes them to respect you deeply. This enables you to get to the Bigger

Reality with them more quickly, thus improving your decision-making and problem-solving skills and results.

How to Be Direct

There are three ways you can become more direct:

- Assume openness.
- Create capacity.
- Establish a common language.

Assume Openness

One of the biggest reasons we're not more direct is that we assume others are not open. We're sure that they'll react negatively, so we judge that it's better to take an indirect approach. But assuming that others are not open oozes with disrespect – it's not believing the best about them.

In my line of work I have to be direct with people constantly. As I anticipate an interaction, I picture the other person receiving and valuing what I have to say. Sometimes they prove me wrong and reveal themselves to lack openness, but I'd rather assume openness and be proven wrong than assume resistance and fail to be direct.

Create Capacity

One of the areas where it's difficult to be direct is in the area of giving feedback. Alan Fine of InsideOut uses the following metaphor to show people how to create capacity. Picture the performer (the person you're giving feedback to) as a drinking glass. The glass represents how much capacity they have to receive input from you. Perhaps they have strong feelings about how they are performing. This would be represented by the glass being three-quarters full. If you try to pour in all your great input, it will end up spilling all over the floor. They will be thinking, "I never want to receive feedback from this person again."

The InsideOut Advantage coaching program trains people to create capacity inside the performer by asking three questions before offering their feedback:

- "What do you feel you did well?"
- "Was there any place you felt you got stuck?"
- "What would you do differently?"

As they pour out their observations to you, their glass is becoming less full and they have more capacity for your input. You have won the right to offer your feedback in a very direct way.

This same principle works in any situation in which you need to be direct. First ask the other person their thoughts on the issue that you need to speak about. By doing so, you not only create capacity, you:

- Gain a clear understanding of where they are coming from.
- Get a clearer picture of how direct you really need to be.
- Discover ways to frame your message that will make it easy for them to understand you.

Establish a Common Language
Here are two examples of how establishing a common language helps produce more directness in a team environment.

Let the Canaries Sing
Niggles are an early warning system similar to the canaries used in mines in days gone by.

The story goes that miners used to take a canary down into the mine with them. Death from oxygen deprivation was a common hazard for the miners. Since canaries are particularly sensitive to lack of oxygen, their singing, or lack of it, provided an auditory oxygen-meter for the miners. When the oxygen level dropped, so would the canary and the singing would stop. That was the signal for the men to hightail it out of the mine shafts. They ignored the communication of the canary at their own peril.

Honoring the niggles of the sensitive people around you is like caring for the canary: you're making sure they can sing. As long as people's niggles are being voiced, you are still safe. When the niggles cease, you may be on the verge of a disaster.

The first could be called "Niggles." We train groups, when they are discussing a decision where everyone on the team needs to be completely committed, to ask, "Does anybody have any niggles?" The team understands that a niggle is a misgiving, no matter how small, that is causing emotional interference. You feel concerned about the implications of the decision that's being tabled but you're not sure it's OK to verbalize your concerns. You may not be able to articulate your concern but there is an instinct inside you that says, "This needs to be addressed."

The term gives team members permission to be direct about their concerns, even though they may seem insignificant.

Directness Test

How direct are you at speaking your truth?

- I tell the waiter when my meal is not the way I ordered it.
- I ask the person who gives me an unsuitable gift whether they would mind if I exchanged it.
- When someone is telling me something they've already told me, I interrupt and let them know, "You've actually told me this already."
- When I am asked for my opinion on something, I tell the person what I really think, not what I believe they want me to say.
- When I don't get a joke, I let the person know I don't get it.
- When someone starts to speak disparagingly to me about someone else, I tell them I'd rather not take part in the conversation.
- When someone uses a word or acronym I don't understand, I stop them and ask them what it means.
- I tell people when I can't hear what they are saying and ask if we can move to a more conducive listening environment.

The second could be called "The Elephant in the Room." This metaphor has been around for many years and it is still a very helpful device for enabling directness. Visualize your meeting-room table surrounded by the members of your team. You see laptops and BlackBerries and reports on top of the table. At one end of the table, you notice four massive stumps. As you look up, you peer into the wrinkled underbelly of a bull elephant. What makes the scene surreal is that all around you, the rest of the team members are carrying on with the meeting as if everything was normal.

This swaying behemoth is dashing laptops to the floor and picking up sheaves of reports in his trunk and sticking them in his mouth. Despite all the bedlam he is causing, nobody says a word about the elephant in the room.

Of course the elephant represents an issue that everyone recognizes but no one wants to address. It is the great un-discussable, the issue that creates interference and causes people to tune out of the conversation.

Teams that understand the language and dynamic of the elephant in the room gain permission to say at any time, "I think we have an elephant in the room." Others know instantly what that means and ask the person to share what they think the elephant is. This small piece of common language allows big issues to be tabled and addressed directly.

Speak Your Truth Productively

Imagine that you have a toothache. It's driving you mad with pain. You go to a dental surgeon, who says, "The tooth is abscessed. It could be removed but it would be very painful. I recommend you just take some Tylenol 3s." What would your response be? You would probably walk out and head for another dental surgeon. The surgeon's unwillingness to hurt you is withholding from you the healing that you need. Left unattended, the problem could go deep and destroy not only your tooth but your jaw as well.

A Hurt That Heals and Is Extremely Productive

You get to the second dental surgeon; she takes one look at your tooth and says, "It has to come out immediately." A couple of hours later she has removed the abscessed tooth. She inflicted significant pain on you, but it was a pain that ultimately healed you.

A Hurt That Harms

A couple of months later you decide it is time to do something about your chronic back problem. You see a young surgeon who seems to be very progressive. He has a bit of a cavalier attitude and scorns the opinions of the other surgeons that you have visited. He tells you of a new operation that he believes will eliminate your pain. Won over by his confidence, you submit yourself to the operation. As he operates, he ends up severing your spinal cord. He has inflicted a hurt that causes harm. You end up incapacitated by his careless action.

Every day, you get to choose what you will do with your truth:

- If you don't speak it productively, you are withholding the hurt that could heal a situation or another person.
- If you speak your truth productively, you administer a hurt but ultimately produce healing.
- If you speak your truth but do it unproductively, you inflict a hurt that produces harm.

What Is Your "Truth"?

Your truth is a lowercase "t" truth. I don't know any human being who has the uppercase "T" Truth. In essence, your truth is your perception of reality. It's how you see the world, yourself, and others. But even though your truth is simply your perception, it is vitally important that you speak it. As you do, you contribute to a Bigger Reality (upper case B – upper case R).

Use Non-Blaming Language

Let's remember the purpose of what you're doing here. You're inviting someone into your world so they can see and feel your reality. You don't want to do anything that will shut them down or trigger a defensive response and send them scurrying back into their own world, taking an armor-clad battle stance against you. You'll never get to the Bigger Reality if that happens.

To avoid this reaction, learn to use non-blaming, non-accusatory language. The essence of this concept is to speak your truth in terms of your feelings and the impact of situations to you rather than assigning a value judgment to the other's behavior. Taking responsibility for your own feelings rather than blaming someone for "making you feel" a certain way sidesteps the defensiveness of the listener, draws them inside your world, and helps them see and feel your reality. For example, it is typically more productive to say:

- "I need to feel heard by you" rather than "You're not listening to me."
- "I felt disappointed" rather than "You let me down."

This is not to say that it is inappropriate to speak about others' behaviors, but it is critical that you do so productively. This is done by using the XYZ approach developed by marriage experts Les and Leslie Parrott. "When you do x, it impacts me in the following ways and I feel y. Is it possible for you to do z instead?"

x =	y =	z =
Pinpointing the other person's behavior.	Identifying the *impact* of that behavior on you in terms that they can understand and identifying the *feeling* associated with that behavior.	Bringing the person to a choicepoint about whether they change the behavior or not.

Do not:

- Blame the person for causing your feeling.
- Judge the behavior as wrong.
- Assign a motive to the behavior.
- Demand that the other person change their behavior.

If you are adept at using "I language" (using "I messages" versus "you messages"), you may take exception when I recommend the XYZ methodology since it encourages people to use the "When you do ..." language. I recommend this approach for two key reasons. First, people (especially men) often get stuck trying to frame situations in "I language." They feel clumsy and end up defaulting to their old habits of assigning blame to the other person. Second, people who prefer directness often feel that statements couched in "I language" are not straightforward enough. As long as blame is not being assigned, they appreciate the direct approach of someone who says, "When you come to meetings late ..."

Naturally, it's important to be aware of your tone when you are seeking to use non-blaming language. You can use all the right words, but if your tone telegraphs judgment and disapproval, the person will feel blamed and become defensive.

> ### Examples of XYZ Language
> - When you come to meetings late, it's an unproductive use of the rest of the team's time and I end up feeling like I'm not valued. Is it possible for you to come on time in the future?
> - When you criticize me in front of the other employees, it's demotivating and embarrassing for me. Is there a way we can have those conversations in private from now on?
> - When decisions like this are made without my input, it's hard for me to own the final outcome and I feel left out of the loop. What can be done to make sure I get brought in at the beginning next time?
> - When you don't give me a heads-up that you're going to be out of the office and people call in asking for you, it makes us look unprofessional and I feel foolish. How can you and I create a system that keeps us credible in our clients' eyes?

Use Humor to Take the Edge Off Your Message

Darlene is a director who works in the midst of a highly political, power-based leadership team.

"I don't know how she does it," says one of the VPs. "She has an uncanny knack of getting our attention and persuading us to do the right thing for our people. She has saved our bacon many times. She has a way of framing the issue in a humorous way. It makes her come across as completely non-confrontational. There's something about the way she does it that makes it feel like we're not losing face. It's pretty easy to say yes to her requests."

I've seen Darlene work her magic. She not only uses humor, she delivers her messages with a warm, authentic smile. This sends a clear signal that she bears no threat to her recipients.

Next time you need to pull someone into your reality, lighten up. Using a smile and a bit of humor does a better job of inviting them into your world than a frowning face and menacing message.

Pull Out Their Intentions

When you speak your truth productively, you are going to have to deal with what you believe about people's intentions. And there are at least three good reasons why you probably don't understand the other person's intentions (even though you think you do):

1 Intentions are invisible.
2 People are different.
3 We tend to assume that others do things for the same reasons that we do them.

Because intentions are so difficult to scope out and yet so crucial to interpreting someone's words and actions, it's important to learn how to pull them out.

I have a friend who approaches conflict situations with the lead-in, "I'm not questioning your intentions, but I need to understand ..." I think that is a good approach, especially if it is true that you have no question about someone's intentions. I do believe there is an even more effective way, and that is to straightforwardly express your thoughts about their intentions. Let me give you three examples.

1 If you have no clue, start by assuming positive intent:
   • "I'm assuming that you didn't mean it to come across this way, but your email yesterday left me feeling shut out of the process. Can you help me understand what you were intending?"
2 If you have a hunch, but aren't sure, tell them you aren't sure:
   • "I'm not sure whether you intended this or not, but my name was left off the list again. Can you tell me why that might be?"
3 If you feel certain of their intent, be careful. You can never be certain of someone's intent until you check with them. Tell them:
   • "When you questioned my integrity in front of the team I began to wonder whether you said it on purpose to embarrass me. I don't know why you'd want to do that, but that's what goes through my mind when that happens. Can you tell me what was going on for you?"

I have found it helpful to assume that the other person is of good will. History has shown me that this assumption is accurate at least three-quarters of the time. I would rather see people in this positive light and risk getting burned 25% of the time than view people in a negative light 75% of the time just to protect myself from getting burned now and again. I lose far less in getting the occasional burn than I would by consistently assuming the worst about people.

> *I lose far less in getting the occasional burn than I would by consistently assuming the worst about people.*

Avoid the Absolutes

Remember to stay away from the expressions "you never" and "you always." Have you ever had someone tell you, "You *always* make us late for our deadlines" (or some other "always")? Apart from feeling defensive or guilty in reaction to this statement, you knew that it wasn't true. Maybe you had messed up a few times, but you weren't personally responsible for the missed deadlines every time! You have been the object of the language of force. Although it may fortify their argument, it typically puts you on the defensive and ends up shutting down your receptivity. You rebut with, "I don't always do that. In fact just the other day I ..." or "You're one to talk! You always ..."

Many of us harbor a need to use superlatives. Let's face it, it feels safer and a lot more comfortable to be able to characterize others fairly simply, feel that we've defined them, and therefore know how to interact with them in any given circumstance. If you leave something open, it could end up being painful.

Learn to replace superlatives and closed-ended beliefs with *data*. "There have been three incidents in the past six months where your material was not done on time. And that has contributed to us missing our deadlines."

Stay Away from "Why"

One word to be careful of is the *why* word. Why tends to put people on the defensive. Perhaps they feel as if their motives are being called into question. So when you speak your truth, try to avoid questions such as, "Why did you choose this supplier?"

Instead, replace why questions with *what* or *how* questions: "What was it about this supplier that caused you to go with them?" or "How did you come to decide on this supplier?"

3 Ask Them to Reflect Back What They've Understood

When you've pulled others into your reality, it is crucial that you check the understanding of the person you've been speaking to. Intelligent people often fall prey to this dynamic: "I'm sure I understand. Let's move on!" Meanwhile, they haven't fully grasped the essence of what the speaker was trying to convey.

This lesson came to us with force in our work with the commercial leadership team of a pharmaceutical organization. Reg, the VP of sales, had returned from a dynamic training intervention. He shared a short, passionate message about what had happened to him and how it was going to change things for the team.

When Reg had finished speaking, we asked him to get every member of the team to reflect back what they had heard. After every member had a chance to do so, we asked Reg to let each one know whether he felt they had understood him or not. It was stunning to see eight very bright individuals not be able to accurately reflect back the essence of Reg's short, passionate message.

This closing-the-loop exercise produced a significant effect: the team members were able to see and feel Reg's reality, and this contributed to a breakthrough of cohesiveness and unity.

How much cohesiveness do you leave on the table when you don't close the loop? How much misunderstanding or missed understanding do you have to go back and repair because you don't take the time to ask people to reflect back what they've heard?

There are ineffective and effective ways to do this. Here are some ways to avoid:

- "Do you understand?"
- "Do you know what I mean?"
- "Am I making sense?"

Ninety percent of the time you will receive the same answer to all three of these questions: "Yes." This gives you little indication regarding whether the person has truly understood you or not.

Here are some more effective approaches to check someone's understanding:

- "Can I ask you to reflect back what that means to you so I know we're on the same page?"
- "How does that sound to you?"
- "What are the implications of that inside your world?"

These questions are more likely to elicit a response that will give you a window into how accurate the person's understanding is. Make note of the third question. The implication question is one of the most effective ways of checking someone's understanding. If they can tell you the implications of your message (rather than simply repeating back your words), there is a very good chance that they have completely understood your intent.

What Are We Really Saying Here?

- Using stories, images, and symbols is the best way to help someone see and feel your reality, and this enables them to change.
- The face-to-face element of directness makes your message more contagious, produces feelings of trust, and sends clear, meaning-making signals to your listener.
- The elements of Pull Conversation enable you to be more effective in virtual communication, not just face to face.
- Being direct earns you people's respect.
- Most people prefer you to be direct.
- To be direct, assume openness, create capacity, establish common language, use non-blaming language, pull out people's intentions, avoid the absolutes, and stay away from "why?"

Want to Make This Happen?

- Copy the Pull Conversation Model (page 18). On a separate piece of paper, illustrate Step 2, "Pull Them into Your Reality," by writing out a story or metaphor that will help the person you are going to converse with see and feel your reality. (You chose this person in the "Want to Make This Happen" section at the end of Chapter 3.)

- If you have done the work of pulling out their reality, it is quite possible you have earned the right to pull them into your world.
- Decide how you will invite them to listen to your point of view.
- Identify the fears that would keep you from speaking your truth productively.

Juice at Home

"Dear Daddy"

In *The Language of Love*, Gary Smalley and John Trent tell a powerful story of a teenage girl who used a metaphor to pull her dad into her world. Kimberly's mom Judy walked into the kitchen to find a note from her husband, Steve, that basically said, "It's over. I've been seeing another woman, and yes, we're involved."

In the ensuing weeks, Judy, Kimberly, and seven-year-old Brian went through agonizing cycles of sadness, rage, and depression. Steve came back home three or four times to pick up mail and clothes. Kimberly confronted him and pleaded with him but could not move her dad's heart to see the pain he was causing his family.

At a counseling session, Kimberly learned about the power of word pictures and decided to write a letter in the hopes of reaching her dad.

> Dear Daddy,
> It's late at night, and I'm sitting in the middle of my bed writing to you. I've wanted to talk with you so many times during the past few weeks. But there never seems to be any time when we're alone.
> Dad, I realize you're dating someone else. And I know you and Mom may never get back together. That's terribly hard to accept – especially knowing that you may never come back home or be an "everyday" dad to me and Brian again. But at least I want you to understand what's going on in our lives.
> Don't think that Mom asked me to write this. She didn't.

She doesn't know I'm writing and neither does Brian. I just want to share with you what I've been thinking.

Dad, I feel like our family has been riding in a nice car for a long time. You know, the kind you always like to have as a company car. It's the kind that has every extra inside and not a scratch on the outside.

But over the years, the car has developed some problems. It's smoking a lot, the wheels wobble, and the seat covers are ripped. The car's been really hard to drive or ride in because of all the shaking and squeaking. But it's still a great automobile – or at least it could be. With a little work, I know it could run for years.

Since we got the car, Brian and I have been in the backseat while you and Mom have been up front. We feel really secure with you driving and Mom beside you. But last month, Mom was at the wheel.

It was nighttime, and we had just turned the corner near our house. Suddenly, we all looked up and saw another car, out of control, heading straight for us. Mom tried to swerve out of the way, but the other car still smashed into us. The impact sent us flying off the road and crashing into a lamppost.

The thing is, Dad, just before being hit, we could see that you were driving the other car. And we saw something else: Sitting next to you was another woman.

It was such a terrible accident that we were all rushed to the emergency ward. But when we asked where you were, no one knew. We're still not really sure where you are or if you were hurt or if you need help.

Mom was really hurt. She was thrown into the steering wheel and broke several ribs. One of them punctured her lungs and almost pierced her heart.

When the car wrecked, the back door smashed into Brian. He was covered with cuts from broken glass, and he shattered his arm, which is now in a cast. But that's not the worst. He's still in so much pain and shock that he doesn't want to talk or play with anyone.

As for me, I was thrown from the car. I was stuck out in the cold for a long time with my right leg broken. As I lay there, I couldn't move and didn't know what was wrong with Mom and Brian. I was hurting so much myself that I couldn't help them.

There have been times since that night when I wondered if any of us would make it. Even though we're getting a little better, we are all still in the hospital. The doctors say I'll need a lot of therapy for my leg, and I know they can help me get better. But I wish it was you who was helping me, instead of them.

The pain is so bad, but what's even worse is that we all miss you so much. Every day we wait to see if you're going to visit us in the hospital, and every day you don't come. I know it's over. But my heart would explode with joy if somehow I could look up and see you walk into my room.

At night when the hospital is really quiet, they push Brian and me into Mom's room, and we all talk about you. We talk about how much we loved driving with you and how we wish you were with us now.

Are you all right? Are you hurting from the wreck? Do you need us like we need you? If you need me, I'm here and I love you.

> Your daughter,
> Kimberly

One week after the letter was mailed, Kimberly was at home in her room. She went downstairs to grab herself a snack.

She put her hand on the railing and slowly descended the stairs. But halfway down, something caught her attention, and she looked up. Standing in the doorway was her father. She hadn't heard the doorbell and had no idea how long he'd been there.

Heartbeats were measured in hours as their eyes met. Kimberly felt that if she looked away, he would disappear.

"Daddy?" she finally said in a faltering voice, her heart leaping.

"Kimberly," her father answered. Then, with emotion filling his voice, he asked, "How's your leg, Honey?"

"My leg?"

"I got your letter."

"Oh ... well, it hasn't been doing too well."

"I'm sorry I hurt you so badly, Kimberly. You don't know how sorry I am," he said, fighting to control his voice. "Your letter came when I didn't know if I could ever return to the family. I felt I'd already gone too far from all of you ever to come back and try again. But your story showed me how much pain I'd caused you all. And to be honest, it made me face the fact that I'd been pretty banged up myself."

He looked at Kimberly and swallowed hard before continuing. "Is your mom upstairs? I'm not promising anything, but I think we need to get some counseling. There's a lot we have to work out."

The result: Two days after Steve came home, he walked into our office for counseling with his wife. And not long afterward, he moved home for good.

Pull Out the Bigger Reality

Performing the Magic of 1 + 1 = 5

*T*HE magic associated with pulling out the Bigger Reality is probably the most difficult concept in this book to articulate. If you have experienced it, you know exactly what I am talking about. If you have not, explaining it to you is like trying to explain the effect of wind on a sailboat to someone who has never sailed. You may be saying to yourself, "Pull Conversation is just active listening on steroids" or "Isn't this really just *Getting to Yes* or some kind of negotiation program like it?" While both these concepts are great, they do not capture the amazing magic that occurs when the Bigger Reality is pulled to the surface.

I am quite clear that there is nothing new in the concept of the whole being greater than the sum of its parts. Most of us know that when our energies are intelligently aligned, your one unit of effort added to my one unit of effort can magically create five units of results. What's astonishing, though, is the regularity with which we can achieve this magic through something as simple and com-

> *What's astonishing is the regularity with which we can achieve this magic.*

monplace as conversation. To see how this is so, just think back to the significant results that emerged from the intelligent energy created by the conversations we have witnessed in this book:

- Unit B doubled its revenue in six months.
- David's marketing leadership team doubled their growth in twelve months.
- Bill saved his organization $1.2 million.
- Fred deVries landed a $7.8-million sale, achieving 403% of his quota.

So let's turn our attention now to the process of pulling out the Bigger Reality so you can more regularly enjoy the benefits of 1 + 1 = 5 in your relationships.

Every Business Tension Has a Bigger Reality

If you are a leader or manager, business tensions are your daily reality. The organization's needs are pulling one way and employees' individual needs are pulling another. And there you are, right in the middle, feeling torn as you try to hold these opposing forces together.

Individual Needs	Organizational Needs
Development Opportunities	Increase Productivity
Work–Life Harmony	Increase Revenue
World-Class Pay and Benefits	Increase Profit
Rapport and Connection with Employees	Increase Performance

For example, on one side you are pulled by individual needs. Jenny is just getting to the place where she is productively pumping out results in her role and she comes to you and says, "I'd really like the development opportunity of working in another role."

"Great," you think, "she's just getting to the point where she's hitting her stride and now she's going to start the learning curve all over again." You feel the tension of being pulled by her individual need for development opportunities and the organizational need for increased productivity.

You have a star sales performer who has been sacrificing his home life to pull in the numbers that have been soft for the rest of the team. He's been on the road for three solid weeks and you want to do your best to clean up some of the toxic spillover that's occurred between his work life and his home life.

Everything in you wants to tell him, "Hey, stay home with your family for a couple days," but there's a monumentally critical client meeting tomorrow and this guy is the only one you know who can hit the ball out of the park.

Do you go with his individual needs for work–life harmony or the organization's needs for increased revenue?

Great business leaders are masters of holding opposing forces in tension. How do they do this? They use Pull Conversation to uncover the Bigger Reality hidden within the business tension. The beauty of tension is that it is filled with energy. Pull out the Bigger Reality, and out of that tension you release productive rather than destructive energy.

The Cost of Not Uncovering the Bigger Reality

One of the largest Canadian banks had a profitability problem. Each of the stakeholders had a different reality. These different realities created business tensions for bank managers.

Head office's reality was, "We want happy customers, happy employees, and bottom-line profit. We will implement a compensation program designed to motivate our branch managers toward customer satisfaction, employee satisfaction, and branch profitability. Any branch with acceptable scores in two of the three areas will be eligible to be rewarded."

The customer's reality was, "I hate having to wait in line." Not surprisingly, waiting in line drove customer-satisfaction scores down.

The Customer Service Representative's reality was, "I hate having lineups of customers impatiently waiting for me to get to them." Not surprisingly, having to face long lineups of impatient customers drove employee-satisfaction scores down.

The branch manager's reality was, "I'm not going to sit idle while two of the three scores that dictate our bonus are going down the drain. I can release this tension first by asking my entire staff to focus on helping move the lineups through and second by assigning more resources to help the CSRs."

Perhaps you've already figured out how this compensation program turned out.

After the program had been implemented for some time, one of the senior VPs shared his reality: "There's only one flaw with the program," he said. "It isn't making the bank profitable." He had a hunch that he knew what the problem was. He called Dr. Peter Hausdorf (his real name) from Inergy HR Solutions to see if he could discover what was going wrong.

Peter began to draw out the assumptions that were obscuring the Bigger Reality. It became clear to him that banks don't make profit by servicing customers in lineups; they make money when customers are sitting in an office getting a loan, a mortgage, or investing their money through a personal wealth advisor.

The assumption that hitting any two of the three scores was all a branch manager had to focus on was deeply flawed. To relieve the tension, branch managers were unwittingly pulling resources and focus away from the profit centers of the bank in order to make employees and customers happy. The Bigger Reality was that, in effect, branch managers were being rewarded for making their branches *less* profitable.

The point of this story is simple: *Pulling out the Bigger Reality in any situation releases intelligent energy from the business tension. The Bigger Reality makes the smartest decisions become apparent and unlocks the best results.* Uncovering the Bigger Reality of wrong-headed rewards influenced the bank to alter its compensation program and achieve all three goals: happy customers, happy employees, and bottom-line profit. The core elements of this

> The Bigger Reality makes the smartest decisions become apparent and unlocks the best results.

skill are illustrated in Step 3, "Pull Out the Bigger Reality," of the Pull Conversation Model. These steps are covered in detail in the rest of this chapter.

3 Pull out the Bigger Reality
- Bring your two worlds together to find the common ground
- Look for a Bigger Reality to emerge – a solution that works for both of you
- Sum it up in your own words

Common Ground
The Bigger Reality

In this chapter you will learn the three critical steps involved in pulling out the Bigger Reality in your personal and work relationships.

1 Bring Your Two Worlds Together to Find the Common Ground

There is one belief, one linguistic device, and one question that will equip you to stand in the middle of your business tension, bring the two worlds together, and find common ground:

- **Belief:** "We are connected."
- **Linguistic device:** The word *and*, used the right way, has the effect of joining your worlds together.
- **Question:** Ask, "What is it we both want here?"

Adopting the Belief: We Are Connected

To the extent that you see yourself as truly separate and apart from others, you will find it extremely toilsome and synthetic to try to find common ground with another person. But if you see yourself as *one with* the other person, even though you may fundamentally disagree, you will find it far easier to discover common ground. As William Isaacs says in his book *Dialogue and the Art of Thinking Together*:

> We may be tempted to say that a given behavior is all "theirs" – I do not have anything like that in me! Maybe so. But the courage

to accept it as not only "out there," but also "in here," enables us to engage in the world in a very different way ... To maintain that it is separate from you is to fall prey to a pathology of thought: that there is a world independent of how you think about it and participate in it.

I have helped many organizations, executive teams, and leadership groups achieve greater levels of cohesiveness. The one simple truth that unlocked trust, collaboration, and synergy in every case was: we are one. That simple reality lies hidden beneath the surface, waiting to be discovered by every fractured relationship, every disintegrated team.

You can choose to let go of the underlying assumptions that separate you from others, such as: "You are my opponent." "We are competitors." "You are the enemy." As you do, you will discover some ways that you are connected, some ways that you are one, some areas where you have common ground on which you can build a lasting solution.

Join Your Worlds Together with "And"

Our language often broadcasts signals that display our intentions. Consider someone saying, "I know you feel it's important to make the changes to the website as soon as possible, *but* I think we need to do some more research to make sure we hit the bull's eye this time." This formulation may be a signal that this person has scant intention of seeking to find the common ground between your world and theirs. They have an either/or mindset versus an *and* mindset.

The word *but*, like a wedge, is a powerful little literary device that drives our two worlds apart and enhances the tension between us. In fact, I've heard of research suggesting that when you join two statements together with the word *but*, over 90% of listeners cannot remember the first statement – they become fixated on the second. For example, when you say, "The quality of your work is excellent, but I need you to increase your output," all that

> *When you join two statements together with the word* but, *over 90% of listeners cannot remember the first statement.*

sticks in their memory is, "You're not giving me enough output." In their minds, the word *but* has summarily eradicated their strength and highlighted their deficiency.

In contrast, the word *and*, like a bolt, can be a powerful little tool to join your worlds together. For example, in the website example cited above, the person could say, instead, "I know you feel it's important to make the changes to the website as soon as possible, *and* I think we need to do some more research to make sure we hit the bull's eye this time. Is there a way for both of us to achieve our goals?"

Other examples:

- "I feel strongly that we need to shut down the line because of our quality problem *and* you feel strongly that we need to push through and meet our quota. Is there a way for us to reconcile these two things?"
- "I understand that you think it's critical that we tell the employees everything we know *and* I believe that there are certain pieces of information that would be inflammatory at this point. I wonder if there's a way to find some middle ground on this."

Notice how, in these examples, the speaker does justice to both worlds and joins them together with *and*. This defuses some of the tension and begins to set a collaborative tone for the conversation.

Practice this. Pick any person you have a difference of opinion with and bolt both of your points of view together with *and*.

Ask "What Is It We Both Want Here?"

Melissa is a pharmaceutical rep who calls on orthopedic surgeons. Her goal is to help make their practices successful by creating value – as defined by them. To create this value, it is imperative that she be able to create relationships with the surgeons. But the Docs have no time for relationships. She constantly faces the refrain, "I have no time to see you. I'm on my way to the elevator. I can give you three minutes."

Melissa has a drug that can help this surgeon, but she can't get him to give her enough time to explain its benefits. Today she decides she will try a different approach: a blend of directness and inquiry that gets to common ground.

"I will only need two minutes of your time, Dr. Naidoo."

What can she accomplish in two minutes? Melissa is going to try to quickly identify the common ground that will enable her to move the relationship forward.

"I want to be very respectful of your time and the busyness of your schedule. May I be direct with you?

"Of course."

"What is it we both want here? Is there some common ground that would give both of us value?"

"I don't know if there is something we both want. You want me to spend time with you. I need to spend time with my end-stage and critical-care patients."

"Yes, that is true. But I think I see something else we both want."
"What is that?"

"We both want more operating-room time for you and less time spent in activities that don't add value to your practice. Would that be accurate?"

"It certainly would."

"I have enabled other surgeons to do exactly that."

"How?"

"It's about the way our drug is applied. The first injection of our pain-relief drug is applied by you, but the two subsequent injections can happen at an injection clinic. The patient is just as happy but your time is freed up."

"I can see that will give me more time in the O.R. but how else will it help my practice?"

"It creates a relationship with the injection clinic that gives them an added revenue stream. They respond by sending you more referrals."

"That makes sense."

"For me to walk you through how this can drug can work for you, I need you to devote an uninterrupted sixty minutes of your time. You probably need to eat sometime during the day. If you are interested, I will bring in some sushi and we can talk over lunch. Will that work for you?"

"If you can keep my patients happy and give me more time in the O.R., of course it would."

"Then I'll set up a time with your office manager?"

"Yes, go ahead and do that."

Finding out "What is it we both want?" has two aspects to it:

- Discovering the things you want that are different from what I want (both of our unique needs).
- Discovering the things we both want together (our common ground).

When Melissa enabled the surgeon to see that there was common ground between them (maximizing operating-room time), it was a relatively easy step to uncover a Bigger Reality (the injection clinic) that would add value to the surgeon's practice and increase the number of scripts she generated within that practice. This is performing the magic of 1 + 1 = 5.

I have discovered that asking "What is it we both want here?" is one of the best ways to uncover the common ground that will release energy from a stuck situation.

But people don't often ask this question. Most often, the conversation gets fixated on what it is we *don't want*. Opposition triggers a fear of either losing something you have or not getting something you want.

When this happens, a common reaction is to cut the issue in two, securing for yourself what you want and relinquishing to the other person what you can bear to live without. This *cutting up of the issue* produces a dichotomy (which means, literally, "to cut in two") that makes getting to the Bigger Reality almost impossible.

Dichotomy thinking cuts issues in half that, if left whole, would drive us to discover common ground. Common ground creates a more fruitful outcome, giving us more of what we both want.

In their book *Getting to Yes*, Fisher, Ury, and Patton describe two children quarreling over an orange. Their solution is to cut it in two. One eats the meat and throws the peel away. The other uses the peel of her half for baking a cake and throws the meat away. Dichotomy thinking gave both of them a half when each could have had the whole of their part.

Common ground cannot begin on the basis of a dichotomy. One of the reasons it can't begin there is because there's a real possibility that "what we both want together" will be something different from what can be envisioned from either point of view in the dichotomy. If *that* picture were to be filled in, it's very possible the result would be something different than either "side" is currently imagining.

Give this a try. Ask, "What is it we both want here?" In essence, that simple question shifts your focus from defensiveness and protectionism to opportunity and possibility. It opens the way to discover the intersection between your needs and the needs of the other person. It reveals a piece of common ground that you can both stand on and build on.

Common Ground versus Lowest Common Denominator

Common ground is necessary for work to make sense and for things to go smoothly. But the notion of getting to common ground can also be scary. You, like most of us, have no doubt had experiences of consensus-building when people were forced to agree to something that someone more powerful wanted. Of course, that kind of consensus is no consensus at all. It is an unhealthy compromise and the only common ground here is fear.

But compromise doesn't have to be a negative thing. The word means "to promise together." It can be a positive step that allows people and organizations to move forward. The trouble comes in when we promise out of fear, path of least resistance, or anything other than *what is it we both want here that will allow us to move forward?*

Another objection is: How can we find common ground when we're so different? Workplaces, always diverse, are becoming more so by the day, with greater gender balance, careers spanning more years, and people traveling all over the world. But this reflects a fundamental misconception about common ground: it's not concerned with what you *have* in common but what you *want* in common. Even very diverse groups may have common things that they want to get out of their work, their lives, and their time together.

And finding commonalities *definitely* isn't about the lowest-common-denominator kind of thinking in which a group manages to squeak out something so insipid that no one can disagree with it but no one can be inspired by it, either; or worse, a cobbling together of a bit of everyone's ideas.

Finding out what we both want is the essence of uncovering common ground and pulling out the Bigger Reality.

This kind of "compromise" diminishes everyone. Finding common ground is about much more than the bare minimum. It encompasses, but goes beyond, what everyone *needs*. If you're just getting your needs met, but not getting your wants met, *then keep going until you get the wants!* Finding out what we both want is the essence of uncovering common ground and pulling out the Bigger Reality.

2 *Look for a Bigger Reality to Emerge*

Mirror, Mirror

An international courier company was experiencing difficulties at its central hub. A labyrinth of conveyors and ramps were set up to feed parcels to the trucks. When the P.M. shift was over, the plant was reconfigured before the A.M. shift began their load-out, to allow for the trucks that ran local routes during the daytime. Everyone knew that as many lines as possible should be "mirrored" from one shift to the next: changing the setup of the majority of the plant twice a day was an insane waste.

The massive expenditure of human energy was a big issue. Bigger yet was the hit that quality was taking. Reconfiguring the conveyors was producing confusion that caused parcels to end up at the wrong destinations. The downstream costs of recovery and the checkered reputation this was giving the company were by far the greatest concerns.

Everyone knew the smartest thing was to mirror the P.M. lines to the A.M. lines. Everyone also knew that it would never happen. Whenever it was brought up, the managers on the A.M. shift said, "We just don't believe it will work. It will cause too many problems." The plant manager knew there was no use trying to force the issue on the A.M. managers. If he did not have their commitment, the mirroring strategy was doomed to flop.

The managers from the two shifts began to practice Pull Conversation. Throughout an intensive process, the P.M. managers stepped into the A.M. managers' worlds and understood their perspective. As they did so, trust began to build. With this increased trust, the A.M. managers began to feel safe enough to share their reality.

"Our biggest concern," admitted the A.M. managers, "is that if we mirror the plant, we'll be rolling from your shift right into ours. Without doing the setup in between, there's no clear boundary between your shift and ours. As it is now, you're already leaving us with a mess. Think of the pile of %*!@ you'll leave us if there's no break between our shifts."

The P.M. managers responded, "Well, we both want the same thing here: to save time by not having to reconfigure the plant and have less misdirects and less damage in the process. What if we guarantee that we'll hold our guys accountable to make sure you start with a clean plant at the end of our shift?"

The conversation went back and forth until the A.M. managers began to believe the intent of the P.M. guys.

What happened next was remarkable. One person banged his fist down in the middle of the table and said, "Who's in to mirror the plant?" One after another, every manager around the table (all eleven of them) thrust their fists into the middle of the table. They looked into one another's eyes and the pact was complete.

The common ground was there all along, clearly visible to everyone. Both sides even agreed to it in principle: "It's in all of our best interests to mirror the plant." But it was never going to happen until the Bigger Reality was uncovered: "We guarantee we'll leave the plant clean for you when you start." And the Bigger Reality was being obscured by a powerful assumption: "You don't care enough about us to hand us a clean plant at the end of your shift." This stands out as a great example of how drawing out assumptions allows the Bigger Reality to come to the surface.

In situations where results are stuck, there is often an underlying Bigger Reality that is being obscured by some powerful assumptions. Many times the key to unlocking stuck situations is drawing out those assumptions.

"True" Nursing Duties

Fogal Street Medical Center was learning how to do Pull Conversation. The group of doctors was about to move into a new building, so now was the perfect time to deal with organizational issues that needed to change.

One improvement that the doctors agreed on was to streamline the reception process. This could be achieved fairly simply, by hiring a junior-level nursing assistant who would receive all patients and conduct the initial paperwork. A side benefit would be that the rest of the nurses would be freed up to do what they were trained and qualified for: the real nursing stuff of taking histories, blood samples, and blood pressures.

There was only one problem: the nurses weren't buying into this solution.

In the Pull Conversation process, the doctors and nurses were learning how to draw out assumptions, how to bring them to the surface so they could be seen by everyone. At one point, the doctors tabled one of their key assumptions: "We believe that you nurses prefer to spend all of your time on 'true' nursing duties." Once they drew their assumption out, they asked the nurses to respond to it. As the nurses responded, the doctors stepped into their world to see their reality.

The nurses' viewpoint surprised them. They reacted to the doctors' assumption not with gratitude but with alarm. What surfaced was that the nurses highly valued the few minutes of chitchat that they had with patients in the reception area before they got down to more clinical issues. This allowed them to get to know the patients and garnered them a great deal of insight. It was also the most social aspect of their work, which they were loathe to sacrifice. "If you take this away from us," said one nurse, "you're taking away our life!"

The doctors now saw the nurses' reality. They had successfully drawn out their own (invalid) assumption and discovered that, in fact, the opposite was true. Additionally, they had drawn out the nurses' (valid) assumption that their personal contact with patients was integral to their true nursing function. Drawing out assumptions played a critical role in uncovering the Bigger Reality.

> *They gained unforgettable insights into each other and came up with a mutually beneficial solution.*

By making their assumptions explicit, the doctors and nurses were able to avoid what would have been an energy-sapping mistake. They gained unforgettable insights into each other and came up with a mutually beneficial solution. Pull Conversation drew their mental models to the surface, stripped away the distortions and generalizations that were based on a faulty reality, and replaced them with a reliable understanding. This is one of the most powerful benefits of Pull: getting to the Bigger Reality recalibrates our faulty beliefs and replaces them with reliable ones.

We discovered an interesting endnote to this case from research reported by Riggio and Taylor in the *Journal of Business and Psychology*. Nurses with advanced social skills perform better than their socially challenged peers. In light of such findings, it makes sense that the nurses in this study would have identified the "socializing" part of their job as *the* critical piece. In fact, it couldn't be separated out; it was part and parcel of overall good performance on their part.

3 Sum It Up in Your Own Words

In Step 1 and Step 2 of the Pull Conversation Model, we stressed the importance of ensuring that you have achieved a shared understanding with your conversation partner. It's no different in this step. Once the Bigger Reality emerges, sum it up in your own words to create a point of joint validation and clarity that will spark intelligent energy and prompt high-performing behaviors.

Finding the True Motives

"Let's kick butt!" was the slogan for Gary's sales initiative to aggressively introduce a new drug into the market. In keeping with the metaphor, he had offered to buy a pair of cowboy boots for any member of his sales team who met the initiative's sales quota – a gimmick that was offered without thought to its effect on the rest of the organization.

To Gary's surprise, other teams were upset. "We're working our butts off, too," they grumbled, "and we don't get any special prizes or recognition." Wanda, the leader of another sales group, was one of the main proponents of this criticism. When Wanda and Gary squared off, a hostile encounter ensued.

"Don't you understand the implications of what that does to our culture?" Wanda said to Gary. "How demotivating it is to other people?"

In addition to her genuine concern about the situation, Wanda was speaking from a well-rehearsed script. In her estimation, her team was always being ignored and shoved aside by the louder, flashier salespeople on Gary's team.

Gary reacted in a lofty, patronizing manner. "If your team was performing, you could get them some nice perks, too. Whatever it takes to motivate my people – it's well worth it. If it ruffles a few feathers, who cares? It doesn't matter."

His attitude only enraged Wanda further and made her drive home her point even more forcefully.

On the surface, it appeared that Gary and Wanda had no common ground. But, in fact, they both wanted the new drug to be successful. That commonality, though, was completely invisible, buried under the disagreement over the cowboy boots and the powerful assumptions they had about each other.

In their Pull Conversation work, assumptions were carefully drawn to the surface. Gary assumed that Wanda was picking apart his incentive program just because she was jealous about his success. Wanda was able to clarify what was really going on inside her.

"I confess the success of your sales team does create a bit of insecurity for me," she said, "but I cannot honestly say that I am jealous of you. My biggest concern is how my team and other teams in the organization will feel demotivated and unfair about the special perks your group gets. I strongly believe things like this can erode away at our ability to be successful as a unified team."

Wanda assumed that Gary didn't care about the rest of the organization and saw them as second class to his sales team. Gary was able to clarify that he did care about the rest of the organization.

"I simply believed that they were mature enough to put my team's cowboy boots into context and cut them some slack," he said. "I didn't believe for one minute that they'd feel slighted by not getting a pair of cowboy boots!"

Gary came to see that the success of the company was bigger than this particular sales promotion. For her part, Wanda was able to see that Gary's motive behind the cowboy boot scheme really was to recognize people for doing a great job. He wasn't out to hurt the other parts of the organization.

Once Gary and Wanda were able to step into each other's worlds and understand what was going on for the other *from the inside out*, they could remove all the stuff that was deeply burying their common ground. Their common ground had been there the whole time, but only now could they recognize it and build on it.

Gary realized that he needed to be more careful about his actions and have more dialogue with others before making decisions. For her part, Wanda realized that in her frustration she'd been caricaturing Gary as some kind of devil. He was human, too. What they both had in common was that their true motives were for the success of the whole company. They could become partners based on that realization.

What Is an Assumption?

An assumption is a belief or conclusion that you take to be true despite the fact that it has not yet been validated. The word *assume* literally means "to take." As we walk into our adult relationships, for instance, *we take* things to be true that have been deeply imprinted on us in our early life.

An assumption can be completely true, completely false, or a mixture of truth and falsehood. The issue with assumptions is that we take them to be true even though they have not been validated and we *rarely* validate them.

Some assumptions are unhealthy and some are healthy. Unhealthy assumptions are based on unreality and healthy ones are based on reality. It's too bad that assumptions have taken such a bum rap over the past several years. How many times have you heard someone state, "Assumptions make an ASS out of U and ME"? Sorry, but here are a few things that it may help you to assume a whole lot more:

- That when others give you constructive feedback, they are trying to help you, not hurt you.
- That most people want to do their best.
- That every person has intrinsic worth.
- That most people don't wake up in the morning plotting how to ruin your day.

But while there are good, healthy assumptions that can improve the quality of your relationships, there are also unhealthy ones that have the power to sabotage.

Where Do Assumptions Come From?

Laura is five years old and she finally gets to go to kindergarten. Her older brothers, Darren and Tyson, are given the (embarrassing) task of making sure she gets to school and back safely. One day, as the three of them are walking by the house three down from theirs, Tyson, with a wink to Darren, says, "I sure hope that monster in Old McGregor's garage doesn't ever get loose. I hear he catches little girls and takes them into the garage and tortures them."

"That's not true, Tyson. Is it, Darren?" Laura says.

"Yup. It sure is. Uh-oh, I think I see him now. Run!"

Darren and Tyson take off running. Laura's little legs can't keep up. She screams in terror as she tries to get away from the monster that she believes is behind her. When she finally gets to school, she is sobbing inconsolably.

Now Laura is ten years old. It is wintertime and she's walking her new friend Kayla home from school in the dark. Kayla lives in the old McGregor house. She can't understand why Laura will never come over to her house. Her excuses always seem lame.

As Laura says goodbye to Kayla, she walks past the garage and feels the familiar sensation. Her insides are shredding. It's all she can do to keep from bolting. In her mind, she knows there is no monster, but in her emotions, she's quite sure he's in there.

Life offered Laura a cruel piece of data and she assumed it (she took it in). Although it is never validated, she believes it in her emotions.

All of us have been imprinted with assumptions. Some are healthy and serve us well: "People have intrinsic worth." Some are faulty and sabotage our relationships: "I need to please people in order to be accepted." We call the unhealthy ones killer assumptions because they bring death to relationships. How do assumptions get embedded in us?

The Assumption Chip

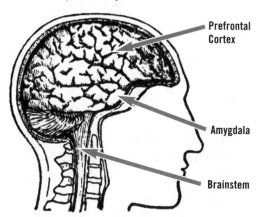

Prefrontal Cortex

Amygdala

Brainstem

There is a physiological explanation for what happened to Laura. Our brains are made up of three main areas. The first is the brainstem. It is only important for those who want to breathe and have a pulse – it regulates those functions.

The second part is called the prefrontal cortex. It is responsible for all the rational decision-making and information processing. The cortex acts like our CPU (central processing unit).

The third part of our brains is called the amygdala. It is a small, almond-shaped organ that acts like an emotional computer chip. It takes in and becomes deeply embedded with all of our emotional memories, highlighting the ones that will be instrumental to our safety.

Laura's amygdala was encoded with a strong emotional experience about Mr. McGregor's garage. This experience created an operating assumption. Every time she walks by his garage, she is flooded with the original stimulus and her body reacts accordingly. Killer assumptions produce self-limiting instincts. Laura values her relationship with Kayla, but her assumption is subverting her values.

Unless you grew up in an emotional vacuum, your amygdala has probably been encoded with a few emotional experiences that created some operating assumptions within you. Some of those assumptions may be helpful to you. Others may be derailing you in significant ways.

The Amygdala Hijack

What do you think of when you hear the word *hijack*? Perhaps words like *sudden, violent, loss of control* come to your mind. These are the perfect descriptors of what happens when your amygdala picks up a signal, in the midst of a conversation, that you are being threatened.

The interesting thing about the amygdala is that it cannot tell the difference between a real or imagined event. When a stimulus enters the amygdala that resembles a past traumatic experience, the *amygdala assumes* that you are in the exact same situation. It secretes hormones into your body to prepare you for fight or flight. Cortisol is pumped into your prefrontal cortex, your sensory acuity is heightened, and your large muscles are prepared for action.

This response works brilliantly for preparing you to wrestle with or run from a saber-tooth tiger, but it is less than ideal for preparing you for a tough conversation with a colleague. Why? Because when cortisol is pumped into your prefrontal cortex, your logical processing faculties are reduced by up to 66%. Perhaps you've had times when you looked back on an argument and thought, "Why didn't I think of saying *x*? It would have been perfect." The reason you didn't think to say *x* is that you were literally stupid in the moment. You were the victim of a sudden, violent loss of control called an amygdala hijack.

But there is good news. If you can recognize you are having an amygdala hijack, you can flush the cortisol out of your prefrontal cortex and regain your logic. Cortisol is flushed out by two things: time and oxygen. So the next time you feel your body gear up and your mind shut down:

Step 1: Recognize it's happening.

Step 2: Oxygenate (the old adage of ten deep breaths is valid).

Step 3: Ask for some time ("Can we take a five-minute break and then come back to this?")

Do Your Assumptions Matter?

Your ABCs (assumptions, beliefs, conclusions) matter as much as anything possibly can. The following story shows how assumptions were cutting a runner's output in half and how recalibrating them doubled his output.

Randy saw himself as a five-mile kind of runner. If anyone asked him about running eight or ten miles, he would decline. Then, one day, something happened that radically changed things for him. He was running on a new path. It was a beautiful day and the river, glistening beside the running path, was breathtaking. He ran up to a gorgeous waterfall, drank in the scene for a moment, then ran back home.

When he returned, his wife called out to him, "You've been gone quite awhile. How far did you go?"

Randy gave his usual reply: "Five miles like always."

"You must have run farther than that. Where did you go?"

"I ran up to the waterfall. It was beautiful."

"You ran to the waterfall? That's over ten miles, round trip!"

"Nope. That's impossible. I can't run ten miles."

They got in the car, each wanting to prove the other wrong, and drove along the running path up to the waterfall. Yes, the five-mile guy had just run over ten miles, without feeling that he had doubled his effort. From that day forward, Randy's behavior was changed. Why? His assumption had been recalibrated by a Bigger Reality. He now saw himself differently, and it turned him into an even better runner. *You realize what you realize*, or, in other words, the things that you realize become your reality.

Do you know how this story applies to you? Do you, like Randy, hold assumptions about yourself or others that are distorted? If you can learn to see yourself accurately, you can double your output in one important area. Which one?

Drawing out assumptions:

- Solves some puzzling mysteries:
  - "*Now* I know why she feels that I'm a control freak!"
  - "Finally I can see why he felt he had to do that."
  - "I always wondered why they didn't want to get together with us!"
- Allows you to interpret and sometimes even anticipate people's behavior.
- Gives you the context you need to understand other people's worlds more quickly and deeply.

Drawing out assumptions can expose and defuse dangerous misunderstandings. Some assumptions can be real relationship killers.

Assumptions are the powerful forces inside people that certainly and silently drive their behaviors.

There they are, as you read this right now, doing their silent work in you and the people around you. They have a subterranean nature. Assumptions are the powerful forces inside people that certainly and silently drive their behaviors.

Family Business

My friend Adam recently drew an assumption out of his brother that was threatening to disintegrate their relationship. Adam's mother, Lila, had three sons, Pat, Casey, and Adam. For whatever reason, Lila favored Pat and Adam and didn't have much of a place in her heart for Casey.

As the sons grew older and got married, Lila occasionally gave them sizeable chunks of money. Pat and Adam assumed that she was giving all three of them the same amount.

But Lila let Casey know that he was not receiving as much money as his brothers. Casey assumed that Pat and Adam were using their favored position with Lila to take away his share and

shortchange him. Picture the resentment and bitterness that festered inside Casey as this continued for several years.

When Lila died, she left the family business to the three brothers. Casey instantly demanded that his brothers buy him out. But it was impossible for Pat and Adam to come up with the cash that they would need to do so. This created what seemed to be an unsolvable dilemma.

One day, on a long car ride together, Adam had the chance to have a Pull Conversation with Casey. He was certain there were killer assumptions lurking beneath the surface between the two of them. His job was to draw them out without shutting Casey down.

As he carefully drew out Casey's assumptions, Adam was horrified to learn how his brother had been perceiving him. But he was able to get past his "self" and step into Casey's world. As he did, he began to see and feel the jagged wound of rejection that Lila's behaviors had inflicted on his brother. He was beginning to understand Casey's reality for the first time.

When Casey began to feel understood by Adam, he became receptive and willing to hear his side of the story. Adam explained that he had no knowledge of Casey's being shortchanged, and Casey began to see the situation the way it really was. His reality was getting bigger. The bigger his reality got, the more connected he felt to his brother. The upshot was that he retracted his demands to be bought out. The three brothers are equal partners in the family business to this day.

Killer Assumptions Derail Smart People

Although some assumptions are healthy for relationships, others are relationship killers. Below is a list of killer assumptions. To determine if any of these assumptions are affecting you adversely, ask yourself this question as you read each one: "Do I *often* come to the conclusion that ..."

- I cannot trust people.
- Being honest will only hurt you.
- It's up to me to fix things.
- Others will let me down.

- If I take the lead I will be rejected.
- I have to be liked to be respected.
- Women will shaft me.
- Men are self-centered and conceited.
- Leaders will take advantage of me.
- Change is bad.
- There is no justice.
- Organizations always take advantage of people.
- To be accepted, I need to show that I'm better.
- People who don't agree with me don't understand me.
- When you don't return my calls, I must have done something wrong.
- If I press, I will be rejected.
- I always get trapped.
- I can't seem to understand – I'm not smart enough.
- I will get left behind/abandoned.
- I have to be forceful to effectively persuade people.
- People always blame me for things.
- Others are more important than me.
- Difference is bad.
- I need to please people to be acceptable.
- Conflict and anger are bad.
- To be safe, I have to be in control.
- Nobody seems to care what I think.
- People are only interested in me for what I can do for them.
- Nothing can be done once you've blown it in a relationship.
- No one understands me.

Looking at each assumption that applies to you, ask yourself, "What impact has this assumption had on my relationships?"

Now book some time with someone you trust who knows you well. Make it your goal to see yourself through their eyes. Ask them to answer these two questions frankly:

- In what ways do you think this assumption has been affecting me negatively?

- From your perspective, what is the truth, or reality, about me with respect to this issue?

One of the most powerful benefits of Pull Conversation is its ability to recalibrate your beliefs and get you to a bigger, more reliable reality.

One of the most powerful benefits of Pull Conversation is its ability to recalibrate your beliefs and get you to a bigger, more reliable reality. Many times we have blind spots that keep us from seeing ourselves accurately. As you pull out this trusted person's reality, merge their frame of reference with your own so you can gain a greater depth of perception about your assumptions and behaviors.

Assumptions Drive Behaviors

Rudy is a young manager who oversees a team of five graphic designers. He is dedicated, bright, and ambitious. It is clear to all around him that he values success and has his eye set on a senior position in the company. Although he doesn't broadcast it, everyone knows he works insane hours.

Although Rudy's personal work is always topnotch, the quality and quantity of his employees' work has become a major concern to his boss, Anjou. Anjou wants him to commit to holding his employees accountable for their output. Rudy assures her that he will talk to every member of his team and make sure they are crystal clear on what he and the company expect of them.

A month goes by and Rudy's department is farther behind than ever. Anjou brings Rudy's employees in one by one to discover exactly what he has been doing to hold them accountable for results. What she discovers is that they have no clue how grave the situation is. It is clear that despite Rudy's dedication, he has not confronted his team about their lack of performance.

Anjou is torn. She is going to have to remove Rudy from a position he seems perfectly suited for. He is talented, values results, and wants to succeed, yet he finds himself unable to hold his employees accountable.

As Anjou begins to pull out Rudy's reality, she discovers that his values are being sabotaged by a powerful life assumption that conflict is bad. Rudy can do anything but confront someone. He will gladly work sixteen-hour days to compensate for their lack of effort, but he cannot and will not confront them. It is simply too painful.

Rudy values success but his beliefs and assumptions are subverting the behaviors that would make him a successful leader. In fact, when assumptions and values collide, assumptions always win out. That's because they hook into a competing goal that is bigger and more powerful than any of your values, goals, and desires. Assumptions hook into your core feeling needs. In Rudy's case, the assumption that conflict is bad was hooked into his core feeling needs of innocence, acceptance, inclusion, and understanding.

His assumption told him that if he entered into conflict he would feel guilty, rejected, excluded, and misunderstood. No amount of success seemed to be worth that. Rudy could not move forward until he challenged this fundamental life assumption.

If you are a leader of an employee like Rudy, you can be instrumental in helping pull out a Bigger Reality that can liberate his energy and help him achieve extraordinary results. Pull out Rudy's reality. Draw out of him how difficult it is for him to confront people. Don't try to correct him or encourage him at this point. Simply see and feel his reality and reflect it back so he's sure that you understand him.

Once Rudy feels understood, ask him to see your perspective.

"Rudy, I feel completely torn. I have no one who is as dedicated, talented, and results oriented as you. But your inability to confront your people and hold them accountable is deteriorating the results of your entire department. Let me ask you, is it the truth about Rudy that he can't speak his truth?"

Phrasing the question in this way helps Rudy see himself from an observer's position. It objectifies his view of himself. Rudy may reply, "No it's not the truth about me that I can't speak my truth. I do that in the relationships that matter most to me. I can hold people accountable."

Then you can pull out a Bigger Reality.

"So if you were speaking your truth and holding your people

accountable, what skills and feelings would you be borrowing from those other areas of your life?"

"I'd be caring more about their overall good than about their comfort in the moment. I'd be focused on how I'm helping them achieve their career goals rather than their goals of avoiding the pain of conflict."

"Can you see yourself doing that?"

"Yes, I can."

"And what specific steps will you take to make this happen?"

At this point, Rudy sees himself differently. He loves to help and support. The Bigger Reality he has discovered is that he can borrow the feelings and skills of help and support from the areas of his life where he is able to confront people and apply them to his role as a manager. He believes that this is possible because he can see the connection between the confrontation and the overall good of his employees.

Suspend Assumptions by Drawing Them Out

I have a friend who is an artist. When a gallery buys one of his paintings, it puts his name at the top of the display area and John carefully draws the artwork out of his baggage and suspends it, hanging it beneath his name so that everyone can appreciate how he sees the world.

Drawing out your own or someone else's assumptions is like this. You carefully draw the assumption out and suspend it, hanging it under the owner's name so everyone can clearly see this viewpoint of the world. (The word *suspend* actually means "to hang under.") Once the assumption has been drawn out and suspended, it can be validated, invalidated, or tweaked to line up with a Bigger Reality.

Drawing out your assumptions so that others can see your mental models is a gift to them. Why? Because it gives them a meaning-making tool – a clear picture of your underlying thinking. It allows them to more accurately interpret your words and behaviors. When they see your assumptions, it helps them understand your motives. You

> *Drawing out your assumptions spares you the pain of being misunderstood.*

spare them the pain of misunderstanding you. Drawing out your assumptions is a gift to yourself, too, as doing so spares you the pain of being misunderstood.

The corollary is that when you draw assumptions out of others, you see their underlying thinking and can more accurately interpret their words and behaviors. This, of course, is a gift to both of you.

How to Draw Out Assumptions

If you are at a restaurant with a friend and it's your turn to pay, you can grab the check and draw out your money quite assertively. "I'm going to get this one" is a completely appropriate approach.

If you're sure it is your friend's turn to pay, you may want to give them a chance to draw out their money, rather than saying assertively, "Will you get your money out and pay for this?"

Drawing out your own and others' assumptions is somewhat like this. When it's time to draw out your own assumption, you can say assertively, "I'm assuming that I ticked you off yesterday with my too-aggressive comments. Is that true?"

When it's time to draw out someone else's assumptions, however, it is generally not fruitful to be as assertive. They may not be as ready as you are to have their inner thoughts suspended for all to see. One way to keep it gentle is to avoid the use of the "assume" word. People don't like to be accused of making assumptions. So avoid saying, "I think you are assuming that I won't be ready for Friday's sales call." Instead, ask, "Do you have any concerns about my being ready for Friday?"

This draws out the person's assumptions discretely, creating an opportunity for them to tell you what they are really thinking. In general, substituting the words *conclude, belief, think,* and *feel* for the word *assume* is a good rule of thumb.

I often use phrases like this to draw assumptions out of others:

- "*Have you concluded* that Fraser is doing end-runs around you?"
- "*Do you believe* we're dropping the ball on this one?"
- "*Are you thinking* that Jen has done everything she possibly can?"

- "Is this process *starting to feel* contrived to you?"
- "You don't seem to be comfortable with this.
  Can you tell me why?"

Inside the mysterious being called the "person" there are four pools in which assumptions hide. If you have the courage to wade into their murky depths you can draw assumptions to the surface. One good thing about killer assumptions is that once they're surfaced they lose much of their power to harm you. Here are the four pools:

- Their anger.
- Their concerns.
- Their opinions.
- Their say–do gap.

The approach to take as you wade into each one of these pools is to *ask a question, listen closely* to the answer, and *reflect back the essence* in a way that will take you down to the *underlying assumption*.

Their Anger

Someone's anger is such a gift for the person intent on pulling out assumptions. Anger is a natural response that reveals the person's assumptions of how they have been hurt or how they feel threatened.

Following is a question and a dialogue process that will take you beneath the anger to the sense of hurt and beneath the sense of hurt to the assumption that is causing it.

"I feel as if something has offended you. If that's true, can you tell me what it is?"

"Well, I wasn't too impressed that I wasn't notified about last Tuesday's meeting."

"Ah, you wanted to be there?"

"Of course! That project has been my responsibility for the past three years."

"No wonder you're feeling left out in the cold."

"Well, how would *you* feel?"

"Depending on what the meeting was about, I guess I could feel left out."

"What do you mean? What *was* the meeting about?"

"Well, we actually weren't meeting about your project at all."

"You weren't?"

"No. Can you tell me what made you think we were?"

"Well, I just assumed that ... Uh-oh, I *hate* it when I do that!"

This person did a good job of discovering:

- The **anger**: "No one told me about the meeting."
- The **hurt**: "I felt left out."
- The **assumption**: "You wanted me out of there."

Once the assumption was revealed, its power to drive misunderstanding was nullified. If you learn how to place one good question and reflect back with an understanding check, you can take the sting out of many misunderstandings.

Their Concerns

A person's concern can be another gift. It points you to their assumptions. It tells you what they assume they are about to lose. Or it can tell you what they assume they are not going to get.

Here is a question that will take you beneath the concern to the fear and beneath the fear to the assumption that is causing it.

"You don't seem to be comfortable with this. Can you tell me why?"

"Well, I'm not too wild about the prospect of your working with Jeremy."

"You're concerned about him or about me?"

"Well, both actually. He seems a little manipulative."

"You're concerned he's going to take over on me?"

"Well, it wouldn't be the first time."

"So you're afraid I won't stand up to him and our family will lose out?"

"Yes, that's basically it."

This person did a good job of discovering:

The **concerns**: "If you work with Jeremy, he might take over."

The **fear**: "The family will not be protected. We'll lose out as a result."
The **assumption**: "Your fear will win out over your desire to protect us."

Their Opinions

Listen carefully to people's opinions of others' words and behaviors. It gives you a clear window inside them. Their opinions will lead you to their judgments. Their judgments will tell you what they assume is right and wrong. With this new knowledge, you can understand the assumptions that will shape their perception of your words and how you need to frame your words to avoid misunderstandings.

> **"You seemed to react pretty strongly to Shelly's compliments about Margo. What's going on there?"**
> "Can't you see it? Margo's blowing sunshine up Shelly's skirt just like she does to everybody."
> "You mean the way she recognized Shelly in front of her peers was manipulative?"
> "Of course it was. She's manipulating Shelly to get her to work more hours."
> "But can she work more hours? I thought she was part-time."
> "Yeah, well, she must be trying to get something out of her."
> "So when I give you a compliment, what do you think *I'm* trying to get out of you?"
> "I don't know. I just know everybody's after something."

This person did a good job of discovering:

The **opinion**: "Margo's blowing sunshine up her skirt."
The **judgment**: "She's manipulating Shelly to work more hours."
The **assumption**: "Everybody's after something."

Their Say–Do Gap

When people say one thing and do another, one of the following things may be happening:

- They are not being completely truthful.
- They may lack self-awareness.
- Assumptions are at play.

Let's assume that assumptions are at play. Here is an example of questions that get to the assumption that is causing the gap between what someone is saying and what they are doing.

> **"I seem to have a disconnect and I wonder if you can help me. I know you've said you want to go out on your own and I believe you can do it. Can you help me understand why you're still working at the job you hate?"**
>
> "I just don't think the timing is quite right."
>
> "You do believe you've got something valuable to offer, though?"
>
> "Absolutely."
>
> "And didn't you tell me that several prospects have told you they'd be interested in dealing with you?"
>
> "That's right."
>
> "So the market is ripe but you can't leave your other job?"
>
> "Oh, I could leave it all right, and we've got enough saved up to weather the first year or so. I just don't know if it's the right thing for me."
>
> "If your success was absolutely guaranteed, is this what you'd want to be doing?"
>
> "It's exactly what I'd want to be doing."
>
> "Do you believe in your gut that you will succeed at this?"
>
> "Not really. I'm a good starter, but I haven't had good success seeing things through. I guess I don't really believe I can make a go of it."

This person did a good job of discovering:

- What the person was **saying**: "I bring value. Opportunity is knocking. I should go on my own."
- What the person is **doing**: Languishing in a dead-end job.
- The **assumption**: "I assume I will fail."

Learn to see a person's anger, fear, opinions, and say–do gaps as opportunities to draw out the assumptions that can obscure the Bigger Reality. Draw out those assumptions by asking thoughtful questions, listening closely, and reflecting back the essence of the speaker's message. Once faulty beliefs are revealed, they can be recalibrated and the Bigger Reality will often emerge and become apparent.

Assumption Signals

Here are a few words you can watch for to discover whether assumptions are at work beneath the surface.

- *Always, never, everything,* or **nothing**. So few things in life truly are always, never, everything, or nothing. When people use this language of force, it can be a signal that there is an underlying assumption, such as, "You won't listen to me."
- *I'm afraid, I'm concerned, I'm worried*. The language of fear can often signal an underlying assumption, such as, "Things won't work out."
- *I can't seem to, I'm unable to. This won't work*. The language of inability can often signal an underlying assumption, such as, "I will fail."

What Are We Really Saying Here?

- Pulling out the Bigger Reality releases intelligent energy, because the smartest decisions and actions become apparent.
- Pull Conversation produces a collaborative mindset that enables us to identify our common ground. Getting to common ground is the key to pulling out the Bigger Reality.
- To get to common ground, use "and" to join your worlds together, and ask, "What is it we both want here that would allow us to move forward?"
- The Bigger Reality is typically shrouded by unverified assumptions and faulty beliefs.
- An advantage of Pull is that is slices through assumptions and perceptions and gets us to reality.
- Another powerful advantage of Pull: getting to the Bigger Reality recalibrates your faulty beliefs and replaces them with reliable ones.

- There are four areas that you can draw assumptions out of: people's anger, their concerns, their opinions, and their say–do gap.

Want to Make This Happen?

- Book a date to do a Pull Conversation with the person you chose in Chapter 3 (See the "Want to Make This Happen?" section at the end of that chapter.
- Think through Step 3 of the Pull Conversation Model (see the worksheet provided throughout this book) and write down on a copy of it or on a separate piece of paper what you believe the common ground is between your reality and what you believe their reality to be.
- Identify the decisions, behaviors, and results you hope will emerge from this conversation (Steps 4, 5, and 6).
- Go have the conversation

Juice at Home

The Best Future Possible

The movie *I Am Sam* is a rich story about Sam, a mentally challenged dad whose bright young daughter, Lucy, has been taken away by the state because he is deemed not competent to raise her.

Rhandi, a woman who is caring for Lucy, is determined to adopt her. She is very focused on one thing: she wants Lucy living with her and not with Sam. She is about to appear in court to tell the judge why she can give Lucy the care that Sam can't.

Sam is very focused on a different thing: he does not want Lucy to be taken away from him. Sam, his friends, and his lawyer are fighting to prove that he is a great dad.

As the court date approaches, Lucy keeps sneaking out of Rhandi's house and going to visit Sam, who lives close by. As Sam keeps returning Lucy to Rhandi night after night, something begins to dawn on Rhandi. One such night, hours before they both have to appear in court, Sam and Rhandi have a powerful conversation.

Rhandi apologizes to Sam, admitting that she had been planning to lie to the judge, saying she would be giving Lucy a kind of love that she had never experienced.

Sam responds, "I hope you're saying what I think you're saying," and Rhandi says, "I am."

Then, as Rhandi turns to walk down the stairs, Sam asks Rhandi if he can tell her a secret, one that she won't tell the judge. When Rhandi promises not to tell, Sam says, "I always wanted Lucy to have a mother. I always wanted her to have a mother. And help, I need somebody ... to help ... not just anyone ... not just anyone. And you're the red in her painting. I think you're the red in her painting."

The next scene is pure energy. Sam is refereeing Lucy's soccer game, starting the players off with a game of Simon Says. Then you see Lucy running down the field approaching the net and scoring a goal. Sam howls with delight, whisks Lucy off her feet, and runs wildly around the field, followed by all the other players.

Rhandi is looking on with a radiant smile. It is evident that Lucy is now experiencing the care and love of the mother that she's never had and the love of the father that she hoped she'd never lose.

When Sam and Rhandi focused on their common ground – giving Lucy the best future possible – the Bigger Reality – the fact that Lucy could be raised by both of them – presented itself immediately. They reached common ground when Rhandi realized that what she wanted most was the same thing that Sam wanted most: for Lucy to feel loved.

Pull Out People's Best Stuff

6

Releasing Brilliance Through Respect

I love the story of the man who had dealings with two British prime ministers, William Gladstone and Benjamin Disraeli. He said of Gladstone, "Whenever I came away from a conversation with him I was left with the feeling of how brilliant he was." He said of Disraeli, "Whenever I came away from a conversation with Benjamin Disraeli I was left with the feeling of how brilliant *I* was." Disraeli probably earned the right, then, to quip that "the greatest good you can do for another is not just share your riches, but to reveal to him his own."

We have explored how Pull Conversations uncover a Bigger Reality and thereby release intelligent energy. There's another key element in the process of releasing this kind of energy: respect.

Respect

There's a scene in the movie *Erin Brokovich* that I'm particularly fond of. Brokovich is at an impasse. She needs that one cricital piece of evidence, that "smoking gun" that will solve the case. It is nowhere to be found until, like a magnet, she attracts it directly to herself. Why did the plant worker offer her the case-winning tip? My theory is that the respect Erin felt for this man energized her to be open to him, and that the respect he felt coming from her energized him to want to make her successful. In this way, respect is both the source and the result of Pull Conversation.

This is particularly important information for those of you who are leaders, because the more power you are given in an organization, the harder it will be for you to get your hands on front-line intelligence. You can only attract it to yourself through respectful, face-to-face conversations.

> *The more power you are given in an organization, the harder it will be for you to get your hands on front-line intelligence.*

Changing the Unchangeable

There was one person in Catherine's department that everyone avoided. Myrna was fifty years old, heading toward retirement, and had worked in the company forever. She handled all the department's bookings with clients and so was an indispensable support person. Indeed, externally, she was actually very courteous. Her customers liked dealing with her on the phone. Internally, however, she was short-tempered, crude, and belligerent. Getting your work needs met through her was uncomfortable, messy, time-consuming, and frustrating.

Catherine was just as horrified by Myrna as everyone else but had the unenviable position of being one of several people Myrna supported. It was clear to Catherine that Myrna was a needy person. So she decided to try paying attention to her for ten minutes every day. Both of them were early birds, so she thought she would talk to her first thing in the day. Maybe a bit of conversation would make the difference. It would be easy.

It wasn't easy, but it did make a difference.

At first Catherine regretted her decision. In her maiden voyage into Myrna's world, she didn't know how to extricate herself as the ten minutes stretched to half an hour. The second day was no better. By the third she was ready to pull out her hair and was questioning her whole strategy. But strangely, on that third day, Myrna seemed a little more human, and Catherine managed to get out of her office after twenty minutes.

And so it went. Every day, Catherine filled Myrna's emotional tank with respect and acceptance. Though she often still cringed at Myrna's comments, she put aside her reactions, determined to keep listening.

Myrna was as grouchy as ever with everyone else but began to *care* about Catherine's work and delivered it on time, and, miraculously, free of mistakes. Catherine began to see that Myrna was more capable than she had imagined. Eventually the short visits became much more pleasant.

Catherine was the lucky recipient of several revelations about Myrna: that Myrna acted the way she did because her emotional tank was empty; that she *did* have competencies; and that she could be funny and even creative at times.

People who genuinely respect others take the time and energy to look for potential that others overlook. They see others for what they can be rather than what they currently are. Life's mad pace causes many of us to ignore certain people. Respect compels some people to do otherwise. They think, "Maybe there's potential here that I missed on my first fly-by," and go back for another look.

Interestingly enough, having another look is what respect is all about. It comes from a Latin word *respecere*, which means, "to look again." Bill Isaacs, in his book *Dialogue: The Art of Thinking Together*, says that respect "involves a sense of honoring or deferring to someone. Where once we saw one aspect of a person, we look again and realize how much of them we had missed."

The essence of respect, then, is *to look again to recognize someone's true potential and to treat them accordingly.*

Blinds Down

I noticed something early in my career that I would later come to call "Blinds Down." When people teaching me a procedure were abrupt, impatient, or patronizing with me, I would begin to stumble over my words and my thoughts. It was almost as if the blinds would go down over my eyes. There I was, a bumbling idiot who couldn't offer what was inside me to give.

As I double-checked myself, however, I came to see that the problem was not me. First, I knew that I was eager to learn and willing to understand. Second, I could see that other people were having the same difficulty with the same "teachers." Third, I felt articulate and bright around people who took me through the same learning process but demonstrated that they valued my thoughts. I ended up being able to understand in half the time.

The difference between these two types of teachers was simple. The first did not show me any respect. The second did. Now, in my speaking, teaching, and consulting, participants by the thousands confirm this phenomenon, telling me that the key trait releasing their intelligence and efforts may be said in different ways but all with the spelling R-E-S-P-E-C-T:

- "He makes me feel valued."
- "She genuinely listens to me."
- "He gives me his undivided attention."
- "He is nonjudgmental."
- "She asks great questions."

> *Respect pulls out people's brilliance.*

Respect pulls out people's brilliance. But as the next incident illustrates, when you treat people with disrespect, you shut down their capacity to offer you their best stuff.

Near Death by Dog Food

Jason wasn't having such a great time at his job. He had always wanted to work in a distribution center and he liked the challenge of driving the forklift. But much of the time he felt unhappy with the atmosphere of the place and the work was starting to feel like drudgery. Still, he prided himself on contributing his best.

One day, things got a lot worse. He was moving some pallets when his forklift nudged a rack piled with bags of dog food. The rack wasn't properly secured, and hundreds of pounds of the stuff came tumbling down, just missing him.

Jason was badly shaken, but thankful to be alive. What shook him even worse, though, was management's reaction. Instead of being concerned about his safety, his manager and the VP over his area were angry.

"How much dog food did you damage?" they asked him – not "Are you OK?" or, "How can we prevent this from ever happening again?"

As Jason recounted this story to me, it was obvious the profound sense of disrespect he felt. What could be more degrading than having your life compared with some bags of dog food and come out wanting?

"It used to be that I couldn't wait to get to work," he said. "I'd come up with better ways of doing things that would save time or money for the company. I'd come in and work overtime just to help my manager out. Now I just do what I'm told and when they ask me to work overtime, I tell them I've got other things to do."

There it was, the ultimate indictment against a manager: "I just do what I'm told." Respect pulls out people's best stuff. Disrespect pulls out their worst.

Person or Thing?

I drive a Saturn. It runs well and gets great mileage. I'll probably keep it. But if it starts to burn oil or give me transmission problems, I will get rid of it. Why? Because my Saturn is just a thing. I only value and respect it for its utility to me. I have no emotional attachment to it whatsoever.

If, over time, you have begun to value people only for what they can do for you, then you've lost your ability to see them as persons and are seeing them only as things. Don't be surprised by the results.

Positive Image and Positive Action

How exactly does respect pull out people's best stuff? By enabling them to see their potential accurately. Your eyes are the mirror people use to see themselves. Whether your perceptions of others are right or wrong, they define them. If John looks in your eyes and sees rejection and disdain, an image of worthlessness is reflected back to him. If, however, he sees respect, honor, and belief, an image of value is reflected back.

Respect – looking again to see a glimmer of someone's true potential – gives you a positive image of a person. As they look in your eyes and see that positive image, it will create positive action in them.

In his essay "Positive Image, Positive Action: The Affirmative Basis of Organizations," David Cooperrider, a professor of organizational behavior, says:

> We are each made and imagined in the eyes of one another. There is an utter inseparability of the individual from the social context and history of the projective process. And positive interpersonal imagery, the research now shows, accomplishes its work very concretely. Like the placebo response ... it appears that the positive image plants a seed that redirects the mind of the perceiver to think about and see the other with affirmative eyes.

You get to choose whether you look again to recognize people's true potential. You get to choose the image that they see when they look in your eyes. In that sense, you also get to choose whether you pull out their best stuff or their worst.

If They Don't Feel It, It's Not There

It's not enough to respect someone; they must feel respected by you.

But it's not enough to respect someone; they must *feel* respected by you.. Unfortunately, the skill of closing the feeling loop to make sure people feel respected is often missed by those who have a high IQ but an underdeveloped EQ (emotional quotient).

Jerry is a new employee speaking to his boss, Raj. Jerry is processing through Point A, Point B, and Point C. Raj has already gone from point A to K – he's got a clear understanding of the issue and knows where Jerry is going to end up. He starts telling Jerry, "I've got it. I've *got* it. You don't have to tell me any more."

The problem is that Jerry feels he needs to process Points D, E, F,

G, H, I, J, and K to feel that he is perfectly clear in his own thinking. Now he feels disrespected.

Daniel Goleman, in *Working with Emotional Intelligence*, discusses the scientific evidence regarding the physical effects on people when they are disrespected or respected. When we experience stress – for example, when we're being psychologically "erased" or simply ignored by others – our bodies release cortisol, sometimes called the stress hormone. Among other things, cortisol is intimately connected to the functioning of the immune system, which is why stressful situations have a direct effect on our physical well-being.

Goleman says that, by contrast, when we're positively engaged, "our brain is being soaked in a bath of catecholamines and other substances triggered by the adrenal system. These chemicals prime the brain to stay attentive and interested, even fascinated, and energized for a sustained effort."

Goleman describes the kind of listening that draws out brilliance as, simply, "being present." When people are present for us, it sets off these positive reactions in our very being. It's easy to see why brilliance is much more likely to be displayed when people experience truly positive regard.

Respect and Reflection

Reflection is one of the best ways to make people feel respected. It demonstrates to them that you value what they *say* and understand what they *mean*.

When light hits a mirror, it bends the light rays back uniformly, showing an image. Reflect actually means just that, to bend back. Your image hits the mirror and is bent back in order to be received by your eyes.

When a person speaks, make sure you understand their reality. Then act as a mirror for them, bending back their message so accurately and convincingly that they instantly recognize their essence in your reflection of them. This is a great form of honor, as the following story, told by Kerry L. Johnson in *Sales Magic*, illustrates.

> When a person speaks, make sure you understand their reality. Then act as a mirror for them.

It seems that a friend of Johnson's was fortunate to have I.M. Pei, the famous architect, as a seatmate on a cross-country flight. This friend was a native of Boston and had always admired Pei's John Hancock Building in Copley Square. Pei's building sits between two nineteenth-century marvels, Trinity Church and the Boston Public Library. Johnson's friend took the opportunity to ask the architect a question.

"You know," he said, "I always wondered why, flanked by those two buildings of magnificent stone and granite, you sheathed the John Hancock Building in glass?"

"Yes. Well, when you look into that glass, what do you see?"

"Why, I-I-see the two magnificent buildings!"

"Exactly."

A Pull Conversation creates a connection with another person's reality by reflecting it back accurately. The art of reflecting makes you someone people trust to *re-present* them to others. Reflecting is at the heart of what is called active or empathic listening. Your goal is simply to reflect back the essence of the speaker's message in your own words. Don't add to the message, take anything away from it, or evaluate it. Just give back the essence so accurately that the speaker will say, "I couldn't have said it better myself."

> *The art of reflecting makes you someone people trust to re-present them to others.*

When you achieve this, you confer on the speaker an immense amount of respect.

But reflection not only makes others feel valued and respected, it also enables them to achieve a state of clarity and perspective about their own point of view. And that, in turn, enables them to give you more brilliance. Remember my story of Adrian deciding to continue with music? As I stepped into his world, felt his reality, and reflected it back, it released his brilliance. He was able to quickly come up with a great decision that has yielded sustained results for the last decade.

How to Reflect

As we saw in Chapter 3, a reflection is made up of three basic components, preferably framed in your own words:

- A *tentative statement*: "It sounds like ..."
- The *essence of the feeling*: "you're angry ..."
- The *situation that caused the feeling*: "because I forgot to call ..."

Following are several lead-ins to use as you begin to practice the skill of reflection. Soon you will find the ones that feel most natural to you.

Ten Tentative Statements to Use as Lead-ins to Reflection

1 "Let me reflect back what I hear you saying ..."
2 "So what you seem to be saying is ..."
3 "If I understand you correctly ..."
4 "So what I've heard you say so far is ..."
5 "Let me see if I'm getting you ..."
6 "I think I'm on track with you. Let's see if I've got this ..."
7 "Let me play this back to you ..."
8 "Do I have this right ...?"
9 "So is your main point ...?"
10 "Can I check to see if I've got this right ...?"

The Tough Side of Respect

Respect is not soft and fuzzy. Letting people off with less than they are capable of doing is the opposite of this quality. Respect looks like the coach who gets in your face and won't let you get away with anything less than your best. It looks like the boss who pushes you and cuts you zero slack because she sees what you are capable of.

Respect and People's Best Efforts

In my years of work at Eagle's Flight, we developed an exercise to show participants exactly what gets withheld from someone who does not respect others. It also demonstrates *why* people withhold respect. After polling thousands of participants all over the world, we grew confident that the data emerging from this exercise were highly accurate.

I would ask participants to think of the best listener they had ever known, someone who made them feel respected and understood. I would ask them, "What are the things this person does as a listener that make you feel respected and understood?"

They usually created a list like this:

- They look me in the eye.
- They give me their undivided attention.
- They are genuine.
- They give me honest feedback.
- They don't interrupt me.
- They challenge my thinking in an appropriate way.
- They aren't easily distracted.
- They honor my time.
- They acknowledge what I say with nods and facial expressions.
- They are nonjudgmental.
- They put themselves in my shoes.
- They ask me questions when something is not clear.
- They reflect back what I say to be sure they understand.

Then I would give them a stack of cards representing all the valuable resources inside them, things like vision, innovations, constructive feedback, and tried-and-true techniques. I would ask, "Which of these things would you offer to your best listener, the person who makes you feel respected and understood?"

"All of them," they would say.

"Now think about your worst listener, someone who does not make you feel respected and understood," I would say. "What are the types of things they do?"

Their list:

- They interrupt me.
- They are judgmental and jump to conclusions.
- They don't give good eye contact.
- They monopolize the conversation.

- They only act like they are listening.
- They are too easily distracted.
- They don't honor my time.
- They answer phone calls in the middle of what I'm saying.
- They don't acknowledge what I say.
- They are not empathetic.
- They ask me questions about things I've already told them.
- They finish my sentences for me.

My next question: "What would you freely offer a person like this and what would you not offer them?"

People would offer four basics:

- Basic information
- Accurate instructions
- Warnings
- Tried-and-true techniques

The majority of participants said they would withhold all their other resources. This means that people who don't make others feel respected and understood forfeit such critical resources as vision, innovations, misgivings, constructive feedback, respect, empathy, enthusiasm, encouragement, and loyalty.

I would say to them next, "Now let's think about someone who makes you feel moderately respected and understood. What will you offer them?"

At this point, people would start offering their innovations, tried-and-true techniques, constructive feedback, misgivings, and encouragement.

"What resources is this person still missing out on?" I would ask.

"They don't get our vision, respect, loyalty, empathy, and enthusiasm. They don't get those things until they make us feel *completely* respected and understood."

Are You Missing Out on People's Best Stuff?

Are you guilty of any of the misdemeanors on the Worst Listener list? Are you oblivious to the idiosyncrasies you are exhibiting? If so, people may only feel moderately respected and understood by you. Our research shows that if that's true, you are probably forfeiting their vision, respect, loyalty, empathy, and enthusiasm.

Think of the implications of this. If they are not offering you these resources, do you think they are offering you their trust? Likely not. Think of the further implications. Take a close look at the resources that they are withholding. Do you notice anything about them? They represent the deepest part of the person, the part that juices and energizes them about their work. If you are not making people feel completely respected, you are surrounding yourself with un-juiced, de-energized co-workers.

The tragedy in all this is that most people *want* to offer you their best stuff. There are relatively few who spitefully hold back their ideas or loyalty. Disrespect and misunderstanding do have an impact on people's *willingness*, but, more significantly, they have an impact on people's *ability* to offer you their best stuff.

> *People* want *to offer you their best stuff. There are relatively few who spitefully hold back their ideas or loyalty.*

Blind Spots

I have a friend who is an authentic, warm, and caring gentleman. He is a Ph.D. who is about as intelligent as they come. When I talked to him about people's tendencies to withhold, he was mortified.

"Now I know why people have not felt free to tell me certain things. I have a hard time giving people enough eye contact. It's just not comfortable for me. People tell me I come across as aloof and uncaring."

Even without an idiosyncrasy like his, you can easily be perceived as someone who does not make others feel respected and understood – especially if you are very bright.

I know a few individuals who are unbelievably intelligent. They are quick processors who get my point while I'm still trying to process it. Sometimes, with a bit of an edge, they say, "I get it. What you're trying to say is *x*." Then they go on to make their own point. They may feel pumped that they've understood me so quickly, but I don't *feel* understood and as a result I don't feel I can offer them my best stuff.

Ironically, a person may actually be very respectful yet, because of an idiosyncrasy or some other personal problem or lack of skill, fail to make people *feel* respected. People can't tell if you respect them or not but they can sure tell whether they feel respected by you or not. It is not enough to respect and understand people. You have to demonstrate the behaviors that make them feel respected and understood. If you want them to be able to give you their best stuff, demonstrate the behaviors that fill them with *feelings* of respect and understanding.

How to Show Respect

If you want to really see people's potential, it's quite possible that you will need to learn how to respect, or "look again." Here are twenty-one behaviors that you can demonstrate to help people feel respected and understood.

1 Learn what kind of eye contact makes them comfortable with you.
2 Use body language that opens them up.
3 Give them your undivided focus, and vigilantly protect the conversation from distractions.
4 Don't jump to conclusions or give in to the urge to judge.
5 Don't finish their sentences for them. Leave generous spaces.
6 Acknowledge them with your body and your voice.
7 Reflect back the essence of their message to demonstrate that you understand their viewpoint.
8 Don't dismiss their ideas, but "look again" until you find the validity in them.
9 Eliminate any patronizing or condescending tones.
10 Challenge their thinking in respectful ways.
11 Show patience while they process.
12 Be inquisitive about what's important to them.
13 Remember and quote things they've said in prior conversations.
14 Listen intently to discover what's going on beneath the surface of the conversation.
15 Use appropriate follow-up as an exclamation point to demonstrate that you understand and respect what they said.

16 Only ask for people's input authentically – that is, if you are open to be changed by what they offer.

17 Step into their world and see the issue the way they see it.

18 Look for the potential in them that others do not recognize.

19 Demonstrate confidence in their ability to understand you.

20 Understand their point of view before trying to make them understand yours.

21 Hear not only what they are saying but what they are trying to say.

Caveat

True respect cannot be manufactured. It's something that "oozes" out of you. Others know that it's there – or not. When you respect someone, they walk away from you with something wonderful sticking to them. If you do not respect people, do some heart-searching and ask yourself, "Why doesn't respect ooze out of me?"

Perhaps you grew up with a dad or mom who, when walking away from an interaction with someone, would say to you, "What a jerk. People are idiots." If you have been encoded with faulty beliefs like this, it's time for you to challenge your fundamental assumptions. I recommend that you do what I did: get yourself a skillful counselor or therapist. Nobody grew up in a perfect environment. Everyone can benefit from some good counseling or therapy. I know many well-put-together people who have done so.

Warning

Are the skills of respect person-specific or universal? There are certain things that leave one person feeling respected and another disrespected. Eye contact and body language are like that. The eye contact I use to make an orthodox Jewish woman feel respected would leave an Arab man feeling insulted. The body language I use with my friend Alex would leave my friend Rick feeling claustrophobic.

How can you know for sure whether you are making people feel respected and understood? Become an astute student of every person you converse with. Here is where stepping into other people's worlds is so critical to your success. It gives you the relational radar to know what's appropriate in each situation. The best measure to use is the quality and depth of the data that people are offering you. If you see someone starting to close off, it's time to alter your approach.

To make people feel respected, manage these Eight Deadly Distractions

1 Scripting while you listen: "Hmmm. What do I want to say next?"
2 Future worry churn: "I better make sure I don't forget to pick up the kids."
3 Past regret churn: "I shouldn't have yelled at the CEO this morning."
4 Present churn: "Oh no, I need to get at that proposal!"
5 Spiritual churn: "I am *way* off-center today."
6 Interruptions: phone calls, BlackBerry messages, people walking in, people walking out.
7 Biological need: fatigue, hunger, hotness, coldness, full bladder.
8 Environmental noise: TV, music, machinery, kids.

What Are We Really Saying Here?

- The essence of respect is *to look again to recognize someone's true potential and to treat them accordingly.*
- If, over time, you have begun to value people only for what they can do for you, then you've lost your ability to see them as persons and you are seeing them as things.
- You can surround yourself with bright people; just make sure you give them the respect that draws out their brilliance.
- Your respect is of little worth to someone unless they feel it. Your job is to communicate it in such a way that they can do so.
- One of the best ways to show someone that you respect them is to reflect back the essence of what they are saying. This shows that you value their viewpoint enough to understand it and repeat it back.

- Respect is not warm and fuzzy. When you respect someone, you demand that they live up to their true potential.
- People withhold their richest inner resources from those who don't make them feel completely respected.
- Respect can not be manufactured. It is something that has to ooze out of you.

Want to Make This Happen?

- Think of an individual whom you have written off.
- Book some time to "look again" to see if there is a glimpse of their potential that you may have missed.
- To understand their potential, pull out their thoughts and their goals and find out what's most important to them.
- Share with a friend what you have learned about this person's potential.

Juice at Home

What Listening Really Is

As we said at the beginning of this chapter, respect means *to look again*. Brenda Ueland, in her book *Strength to Your Sword Arm*, illustrates the transformational effect that looking again can have on a friend.

Recently I saw a man I had not seen for twenty years. He was an unusually forceful man and had made a great deal of money. But he had lost his ability to listen. He talked rapidly and told wonderful stories and it was just fascinating to hear them. But when I spoke – restlessness: "Just hand me that, will you? ... Where is my pipe?" ...

I said to myself: "He has been under a driving pressure for years. His family has grown to resist his talk. But now, by listening, I will pull it all out of him. He must talk freely and on and on. When he has been really listened to enough, he will grow tranquil. He will begin to want to hear me."

And he did, after a few days. He began asking me questions. And presently I was saying gently: "You see, it has become hard for you to listen."

He stopped dead and stared at me. And it was because I had listened with such complete, absorbed, uncritical sympathy, without one flaw of boredom or impatience, that he now believed and trusted me, although he did not know this.

"Now talk," he said. "Tell me more about that. Tell me all about that." ...

... Unless you listen, people are wizened in your presence; they become about a third of themselves. Unless you listen, you can't know anybody. Oh. You will know facts and what is in the newspapers and all of history, perhaps, but you will not know one single person. You know, I have come to think listening is love, that's what it really is.

7

Juice Your Environments

Understanding the Five Drivers of Engagement

*M*ANAGERS in your organization face a choicepoint many times a day: "I've got sixty minutes of unscheduled time. Do I do something that will make me 10% more productive, or do I take ten minutes with each of my six employees and do something that will make each of them 10% more productive?" You do the math. How your managers answer that question determines the future of your company. Unfortunately, most managers get the answer wrong, believing their primary role is to execute technical tasks versus releasing energy in their employees.

There is one simple but brilliant activity that great managers do that enables them to know exactly what is required to energize an employee: they ask.

There is one simple but brilliant activity that great managers do that enables them to know exactly what is required to energize an employee: **they ask.** They actually sit with their employees and ask, "You and I both want the same thing. We both want you to feel completely energized at work. Can I ask you what you need to feel completely energized?"

Most managers believe they could never have this conversation with their employees. They ask: "Wouldn't it create a set of expectations that couldn't be fulfilled? Wouldn't we be setting the employee up for disappointment and ourselves for failure?"

In this chapter you will learn a simple, systematic conversation that you can have with your employees to uncover the drivers that energize and engage them on the job.

Intelligent Listening

Kathy Bardswick (her real name) has a bone-deep credo: "It's not just about the results, it's how you get the results." Building relationships and getting things done for employees is a big part of achieving bold results that go beyond the bottom line. She has a delightful obsession with organizational culture.

When Kathy stepped into the role of president and CEO at the Co-operators Group, in 2002, Canada's largest Canadian-owned insurance company's results were suffering.

Connecting with Employees

So Kathy went to work, demonstrating one of her most striking abilities: to connect with employees deeply and quickly. Other Co-operators leaders have commented to me, "She gets on the elevator with someone on the sixth floor and by the time they reach the bottom floor the person is telling her about her daughter's challenges at school or what's happening on the job." Onlookers are astonished by how quickly and fully people open up to her. But there is a reason why.

When Kathy converses with you, she fully engages you. She gives you her undivided attention, remembers your name, and listens keenly to what's important to you.

The way Kathy listens meets a deep need inside people. But she goes far beyond just listening. In the first quarter of her role at the helm of The Co-operators, Kathy conducted intimate town-hall meetings all across Canada, candidly asking employees what was and what wasn't working. Through her influence, suggestion after suggestion was addressed by managers, which was a clear indication to staff that she was listening to them and valuing their comments. Just recently a manager remarked to me, "We couldn't believe the long list of things that got implemented out of those town-hall meetings!" The organizational energy level was shifting as people began to feel supported, valued, and inspired by the efforts of the leadership team. And town-hall meetings continue to occur regularly in every part of the corporation.

And Kathy also implemented an engagement survey for all staff measuring what staff say about the company, how engaged they are in achieving results, and their likelihood of staying with the company. Weaker areas were addressed and results soared to the point that a full 75% of the company rate themselves as "engaged" and the company has been named one of Canada's Top 50 Companies. Predictably, staff retention numbers continue to excel as the company boasts a voluntary turnover rate of only 4–5%. Financially, the last two years have been the strongest in the history of The Co-operators. The 2005 financial report states:

> Consolidated revenues were solid again in 2005 at $2.7 billion, up from a record $2.6 billion in 2004. Consolidated pre-tax earnings were down 5.1 per cent to $254.4 million. Total capital and surplus reached $1.4 billion, up 13.6 per cent from the previous year and assets grew by 8.4 per cent to $6.6 billion. No small achievements in a mature industry where 1 to 2 per cent growth is normal.

Leaders like Kathy create a wave of optimism that ripples through the workforce. Employees with a cynical wait-and-see attitude begin to witness that their input is followed up with action and positive change. When employees feel their emotional needs are being met, something amazing happens. Cynicism and suspicion are displaced with hope and trust. Higher levels of performance are a natural outcome.

Everyone plays a role in creating an energy-filled environment, but "leaders drive the climate," as Daniel Goleman says in *Primal Leadership*. He adds that "50–70% of how employees perceive their organization's climate can be traced to the actions of one person: the leader."

I have witnessed this powerful phenomenon with leaders like the late Skip LeFauve (real name) at Saturn and Arthur Labbatt (real name) at Trimark. Skip made a point of sitting with employees in the cafeteria, asking them for their thoughts and suggestions and taking appropriate action where he could. He brought a nice blend of inquiry and directness to the table. Saturn employees frequently cited Skip's blend of soft and hard skills as one of the primary sources of the company's energy-filled environment.

Arthur Labbatt engaged with Trimark employees, asking them about their families, returning to them weeks later and still remembering their kids' names and checking back on the situations the employees had described.

What creates a highly engaged employee? Towers Perrin surveyed 41,000 employees in medium to large organizations in the U.S. and Canada to find out. The number-one reason was, "My leaders take an interest in me as a person."

Employees don't want to be viewed as so much corporate chattel. Pull Conversation, conducted face to face, is a powerful signal to them that you are interested in each one of them as a person. But if you're not naturally wired like a Kathy, a Skip, or an Arthur Labbatt, how do you know what to ask in an engagement conversation? There's so much material out there on engagement. Is there a shorthand engagement system that will reliably get results?

The Five Drivers of Engagement

For years I've been on a quest to discover which core emotional needs are the most critical to people in the workplace. I wanted a list that would be simple to remember yet cover off all the most important emotional needs that engage people. Standing on the shoulders of some of the thought pioneers of the last decade, I have identified five core drivers that matter most to employees. These Five Drivers produce the highest levels of organizational energy and unlock employees' ability to offer what they want to offer in their jobs – their best stuff – their discretionary effort. Here are those drivers, framed as statements that employees wish they could make at the end of each work day:

1 I Fit.
2 I'm Clear.
3 I'm Supported.
4 I'm Valued.
5 I'm Inspired.

Can you imagine what it would be like for employees to be able to utter these statements as they drive home from work at night? "I really fit in my role. I'm crystal clear on what's expected of me." Imagine an employee turning to the person next to them on their commute home and saying, "I feel completely supported by my manager." Or imagine overhearing your employee say to their friends at dinner, "The people I work with really value me," or, "My work environment inspires me."

When employees start to make statements like these, engagement and results naturally follow. Here are some of the statements leaders have offered us after focusing on the Five Drivers for six months:

"We've cut our credits and returns in half."
"For the first time in I don't know how long, I've got
    employees singing out on the production line."
"There were several people who had their résumés polished up.
    None of them are looking any more."

Let's examine the specific elements of the Five Drivers that can produce engagement and results for your organization:

I Fit
My role is a good match for my talents.
My role is a good match for my interests.
I fit in well with my team. I feel I belong here.
I feel safe in my current role, both emotionally and physically.

I'm Clear
I'm crystal clear on the outcomes and goals that are
    expected of me.

I'm clear on the big picture and how I contribute to it.

I'm clear on how my manager feels about my progress.

I feel understood by those around me. I experience no unnecessary friction due to misunderstanding.

I'm Supported

I feel equipped with all the resources I need to succeed: time, training, tools, and systems.

My manager "has my back," supporting me and going to bat for me when I need it.

I have the freedom and authority to do what I'm responsible to do.

I'm getting the growth opportunities and challenges that are important to me.

I'm Valued

I feel valued as a person, not as a tool or an asset.

I feel recognized and appreciated for my contribution.

I feel I am being treated fairly.

My leaders listen to me in a way that makes me feel completely understood.

I'm Inspired

I clearly see the link between my day-to-day activities and the grander purpose of my organization.

I am being held accountable to achieve great results.

My colleagues and leaders walk the talk.

The passion of my colleagues inspires me to drive for more aggressive goals.

If you've got an employee who ...

- Is doing what she's talented and motivated to do ...
- Is clear on what's expected of her and understands how her part fits into the big picture ...
- Has all the resources and support she needs to succeed ...
- Feels recognized, valued, and appreciated ...
- Is doing meaningful work and feels successful ...

... then you've got someone who is highly energized, highly engaged, and highly productive.

The Five Drivers Move Employees into Desired States of Being

But you may well ask, "Why are the Five Drivers so vital to employees? Aren't they just five ordinary wants and needs?" Each of these drivers represents a much deeper desired state of being that is crucial to the release of energy in employees. A state of being is more than just a feeling – it is a pervasive emotional condition that affects a person's entire being. For example, "My manager recognized my contribution" is a feeling – "I am significant here" is a state of being. "I've been given the authority to do my job" is a feeling – "I experience freedom here" is a state of being.

There are five main states that people love and need to be in.

- A State of **Purpose**
- A State of **Freedom**
- A State of **Significance**
- A State of **Belonging**
- A State of **Security**

If denied these states of being, employees become depleted of their energy and find it increasingly difficult to offer their engagement and discretionary effort.

The Five Drivers of engagement enable people to move into these five crucial states of being.

The Five Drivers and the States of Being They Move People Into	
Drivers	**States of Being**
I Fit	Belonging
I'm Clear	Security
I'm Supported	Freedom
I'm Valued	Significance
I'm Inspired	Purpose

Why Emotional Needs Matter

Jim Letwin (his real name), the CEO of Jan Kelley Marketing, holds up a pack of Excel gum and asks his audience, "Why do people lay down a buck to buy this pack of Excel? What are they buying? Gum base? Soybean oil? Aspartame?"

People shake their heads.

"What *are* they buying then?" Jim asks.

Someone from the audience confidently shouts out, "Fresh breath."

"Nope," Jim responds. "What they are really buying is *social acceptance.*"

Jim's got a great point. People make their buying decisions based on the *emotional payoff* they will derive from the purchase. We are moved toward pleasurable emotions and away from unpleasurable ones. In this way, emotions are what move us out into action. In fact, that is what emotion means: "to move out."

- When Ian buys insurance, he's not paying for a policy, he's paying for peace of mind.
- When Valerie buys a Volvo, she's not paying for an automobile, she's paying for a feeling of security.
- When Henry buys a Harley, he's not paying for a motorcycle, he's paying for a feeling of respect. (After all, there's no other motorcycle in the world that will allow a fifty-five-year-old accountant with a set of black leathers and a fake ponytail to ride through town and get the head-turning respect he is enjoying. He doesn't get that when he walks down the corridors of his office.)

One of the key learnings here is that many managers deal with employees on the level of fresh breath (surface need) when what really drives the employee's behavior is social acceptance (core emotional need). A friend of mine, Pauline Curtis (real name), asks groups of managers, "What are the types of things you do to recognize your employees?" Managers create a list that looks like this: bring in pizza, send them on a course, give out movie passes, give a weekend-away coupon. Then she asks employees, "How would you like your manager to recognize you?" Employees create a list that looks like this: spend time with me, give me a personal word of thanks, write me a personal note telling me in specific terms how my contribution has helped the company, talk about how good I am in front my peers.

Pauline's point? We assume that employees will feel recognized if we give them stuff despite the fact that what makes *us* feel most recognized is a meaningful interaction with our boss that meets our core emotional needs.

What Is Most Important to Employees?

Significant emerging research has revealed some critical discoveries. We've learned what creates the most **highly engaged** organization from Towers Perrin, BlessingWhite, and Hewitt. We've learned what creates the most **highly productive** workforce from the Gallup Organization. We've learned what creates the most **highly effective** leaders from Daniel Goleman and other Emotional Intelligence researchers. We've learned what creates the most **highly change-adaptive** employees from John Kotter. And finally, we've learned what creates the most **highly performing** employees from the Corporate Leadership Council.

The results of each of these studies are fascinating, but if you view them as a whole and begin to connect the dots, an amazing realization coalesces: *What matters to employees more than anything else at work is feelings.* We call them core emotional drivers. Consider the following five examples:

> What matters to employees more than anything else at work is feelings. We call them core emotional drivers.

Feelings Create Highly Engaged Employees

After surveying more than 40,000 employees in the U.S. and Canada in medium to large organizations, Towers Perrin discovered what attracts, retains, and engages employees. Generally speaking, employees are attracted by pay and benefits, retained by opportunities for development, and engaged by how they feel on the job. What's interesting is that each of Towers Perrin's top ten drivers of employee engagement is instrumental in producing

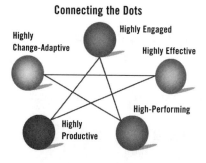

Connecting the Dots

Highly Change-Adaptive

Highly Engaged

Highly Effective

High-Performing

Highly Productive

feelings inside employees. Beside each of the Towers Perrin top ten, we've bracketed the feeling that is produced.

1 Senior management has sincere interest in employees' well-being. (**I'm Valued**)
2 Company provides challenging work. (**I'm Inspired**)
3 Employees have appropriate decision-making authority. (**I'm Supported**)
4 Company cares a great deal about customer satisfaction. (**I'm Inspired**)
5 Employees have excellent career opportunities. (**I fit, I'm Valued, and I'm Supported**)
6 Company has a reputation as a good employer. (**I'm Inspired**)
7 Employees work well in teams. (**I Fit and I'm inspired**)
8 Employees have resources needed to perform jobs in a high-quality way. (**I'm Supported**)
9 Employees have appropriate decision-making input. (**I'm Valued**)
10 Senior management communicates clear vision for long-term success. (**I'm Clear and I'm Inspired**)

Feelings Create Highly Productive Employees

After surveying over two million employees, the Gallup Organization has discovered the twelve elements required for an organization to be highly productive in terms of revenue, profitability, customer loyalty, and employee retention. Interestingly enough, each of the elements produces a specific feeling inside employees. Beside each of the Gallup Q12, we've bracketed the feeling that is produced inside employees.

1 I know what is expected of me at work. (**I'm Clear**)
2 I have the materials and equipment I need to do my work right. (**I'm Supported**)
3 At work, I have the opportunity to do what I do best every day. (**I Fit**)
4 In the last seven days, I have received recognition or praise for doing good work. (**I'm Valued**)

5 My supervisor or someone at work seems to care about me as a person. **(I'm Valued)**

6 There is someone at work who encourages my development. **(I'm Supported)**

7 At work, my opinions seem to count. **(I'm Valued)**

8 The mission/purpose of my company makes me feel that my job is important. **(I'm Inspired)**

9 My associates (fellow employees) are committed to doing quality work. **(I'm Inspired)**

10 I have a best friend at work. **(I Fit)**

11 In the last six months, someone at work has talked to me about my progress. **(I'm Clear and I'm Supported)**

12 This past year, I have had opportunities at work to learn and grow. **(I'm Valued, I'm Supported, I'm Inspired)**

Gallup's study conclusively shows that how employees feel affects the bottom line. Managers who create an environment where these twelve elements (and by extension, the five feelings) are present are *50% more likely* to deliver on *customer loyalty* and *44% more likely* to produce *above-average profitability*.

Feelings Create Highly Change-Adaptive Employees

As discussed earlier in this book, change expert John Kotter of Harvard University recognizes the critical role of feelings in enabling employees to embrace change. Kotter has discovered that trying to get people to embrace change by appealing to their thinking is unproductive. The common approach used to be, "Give them enough analysis and they'll think differently. If they think differently they will engage in change." Kotter's research has shown, however, that the most effective approach is not analyze, think, change but *see, feel, change.* When people see something powerfully modeled, it evokes within them a feeling that enables them to readily embrace change. In short, help people feel right, and they can change.

> *When people see something powerfully modeled, it evokes within them a feeling that enables them to readily embrace change.*

Highly Effective Leaders Create Feelings

Emotional intelligence experts Goleman, Boyatzis, and McKee put it this way, in their book *Primal Leadership*: "The fundamental task of leaders, we argue, is to prime good feelings in those they lead. At its root then, then, the primal job of leadership is emotional. Great leadership works through the emotions."

In addition, it is emotional intelligence (EQ), the ability to identify and manage your own feelings and the feelings of those you work with, that has the greatest impact on making leaders highly effective with their employees.

High Feelings Create High-Performing Employees

In its *Best Practices Research 2002*, the Corporate Leadership Council studied 19,000 employees over seven industries in twenty-nine countries. Their mission was to uncover the drivers that produced the highest levels of performance in organizations. Once again, each of the drivers is responsible for creating certain feelings inside employees. Beside each of the CLC drivers, we've bracketed the feeling that is produced.

- Working on the things you do best can increase performance by up to 28%. **(I Fit)**
- Employee understanding of their performance standards can increase performance by up to 36%. **(I'm Clear)**
- A culture with good internal communication can increase performance by up to 34%. **(I'm Clear)**
- Engagement in on-the-job development opportunities can increase performance by up to 28%. **(I'm Supported)**
- An environment of risk-taking can increase performance by up to 38%. **(I'm Supported and I'm Inspired)**
- Emphasizing an employee's performance strengths can increase performance by up to 36%. **(I'm Valued)**
- Belief that a manager is knowledgeable about an employee's performance can increase performance by up to 30%. **(I'm Valued)**

We Feel First and Think Next

But why are *feelings* so important for engaging people? Why not thoughts, facts, figures, or physical commodities? Brain researchers have discovered that all data entering the prefrontal cortex (the logical, decision-making center of the brain) are first filtered through the amygdala (the emotional center of the brain). In short, we humans feel first, *then* we think. That means people's first response to you is an emotional one. As they interact with you, they are internally assessing, "Do I feel put down? Respected? Listened to? Patronized?"

Furthermore, we have learned that when people think back on their interactions with you, they first remember how you made them feel and only after that do they remember the thoughts and commodities that may have passed between you.

"Soft" Feelings Drive Hard Results

People's emotional
needs drive their
decisions.

People's emotional needs drive their decisions. In fact, *their behaviors can best be understood as an attempt to get their emotional needs met.* If this is true, then the most important thing you can do as a leader is create an environment where each of your employees' core emotional needs is being met.

Marcus Buckingham and Curt Coffman make a strong suggestion in their book *First, Break All the Rules*: "It would be [most] efficient to identify the few emotions you want your employees to feel and then to hold your managers accountable for creating these emotions." The emotions become the outcomes that the manager is primarily responsible for.

Why is the creation of emotional engagement the most important thing a manager can do? Because "emotional engagement is four times more valuable than rational engagement in driving employee effort," says the Corporate Leadership Council in their 2004 Employment Engagement Survey. Following is a comparison of emotional and rational engagement.

Rational Engagement	Emotional Engagement
Engaging the **minds** of your employees	Engaging the **hearts** of your employees
"I understand the organization's strategy and how I contribute to it"	"The excellence of my colleagues inspires me to strive for more aggressive goals"
The **skill** to do more	The **will** to do more
Big-picture understanding, clarity of expectations, connection to financial, developmental, or professional rewards	Feelings of purpose, pride, meaning, inspiration, and loyalty

How do you know what to do to engage an employee emotionally? As I said above, you ask. You sit with them and say, "You and I both want the same thing: for you to be able to feel completely energized in your job. Can I ask you a few questions to find out what makes you completely energized on the job?"

Ask the question, then do what you can to give your employees the feelings of fit, clarity, support, value and inspiration. The beauty of these five simple drivers is that they produce both rational *and* emotional engagement. When that happens, there are some significant payoffs for you and for your company.

Met Needs Pay Big Dividends

Canadian Tire Financial Services (CTFS) has evolved into a powerhouse. It started out, in 1961, as Midland Shoppers Credit Limited. In 1968 Midland became a subsidiary of Canadian Tire and was renamed Canadian Tire Acceptance Limited. In 2002 the company name changed to Canadian Tire Financial Services. In its early years the company was small and had a relatively small stake in the financial industry.

By 2004, CTFS had leapfrogged the competition to take a 5% share of the bank card market, the largest of any Canadian retailer. What was the key factor that enabled CTFS to achieve this level of success? Their ability to systematically ingrain the belief within their leadership team that when employees feel a certain way, they will achieve significant results.

The Story

In 1995, when Tom Gauld (real name) was promoted from VP to president of CTFS, he was up against three key players, Eaton's, Sears, and Hudson's Bay Company – all large Canadian retailers and financial-service companies with proprietary store cards. Canadian Tire and Eaton's were the smallest of the four. Each player faced the same marketplace and had the same opportunity to choose strategies, including the opportunity to issue MasterCard. The strategies of each of these public companies were publicly available. In 1995, CTFS became the first non-deposit-taking financial institution worldwide to launch a MasterCard.

By 2004, Eaton's had left the game, having sold their credit card company. Since 1995, the Bay had reported receivables growth of 20-30%; Sears had reported receivables growth of 20–30%; CTFS had reported receivables growth of over 200%. Following is a list of the other impressive results that come from building an energy-filled culture.

Sustained Results
- CTFS is now the second largest MasterCard issuer in Canada next to Bank of Montreal.
- In 2004, CTFS was voted best call center in North America for the third time in five years by Service Quality Measurement (SQM) Group, based on a benchmarking study of 203 contact centers in North America.
- Customer attrition has improved from 18% in 2000 to 12% in 2004.
- Contact center employee attrition is only 11% compared with SQM's 2004 benchmark of 24%.
- None of CTFS's twenty-five directors has left voluntarily in four years.
- CTFS was also recognized by SQM for the highest Employee Satisfaction in North America in 2004 for the fourth time in five years.

Creating Highly Engaged Employees
Tom Gauld and his leadership team have created a group of highly engaged employees.

CTFS's employee-satisfaction results have shown a high degree of employee commitment. The recent 2004 employee survey results revealed a strong emotional connection which, CTFS leadership believes, drives the rest of the scores. In the survey area "Identify with Company," CTFS scored an average of 3.6 out of 4 compared with a 3.0 out of 3.3 norm. On "Confidence in Leadership," they scored a 3.5 out of 4, compared with a 2.7 out of 3.0 norm. Overall, CTFS scored more than 16% higher than the norms.

How do the Five Drivers show up within CTFS? Consider:

- A Values-Based Culture: CTFS has created a culture where people eat, sleep, and breathe their values (honesty, integrity, respect, and dignity). Employees use the statement of values to determine how to handle situations and to hold one another accountable. This creates an *I'm Inspired* feeling inside employees.

- Outstanding Leadership: CTFS prides itself on its team of outstanding leaders, reinforcing them through significant leadership training, clearly defined and integrated leadership expectations, and systematic 360° feedback. This creates an *I'm inspired* feeling inside employees.

- A Performance Culture: "We are success driven – creating a performance culture while promoting personal fulfillment is at the heart of what we do every day." This creates *I'm Valued* and *I'm Inspired* feelings inside employees.

- Equipping Employees Who Deliver Quality Results: CTFS has invested in the best systems and processes to equip employees with the clarity and tools that they need to achieve their goals. This creates *I'm Clear* and *I'm Supported* feelings inside employees.

- A People-Centered Culture: Much care and focus has been invested inside CTFS to maintain an environment in which team members are cared for as people versus corporate furniture. I've talked to many of their people, and they tell me that it feels good to come to work at CTFS. This creates an *I'm Valued* feeling inside employees.

- Flat Organizational Structure: Tom Gauld has remained true to his determination to keep the organization free of unnecessary organizational levels. Between the CEO and the employee there will only ever be three layers of management. This creates *I'm Clear* and *I'm Supported* feelings inside employees.

- Satisfied Customers: CTFS has stuck with their great customer loyalty programs instead of continually changing them as some of their competitors have done. The Customers for Life philosophy is deeply ingrained throughout a company that is centered on customer-service excellence. CTFS also clearly recognizes that committed, satisfied employees result in satisfied customers. One of the reinforcers of this is the Customers for Life award, which is presented monthly to a CTFS employee who has gone the extra mile for a customer; winners are honored by the president and receive an extra day of vacation. This creates *I'm Valued* and *I'm Inspired* feelings inside employees.

The Bottom Line

CTFS has achieved a strong success story based on a uniquely blended foundation of a highly effective cultural environment and sustained business processes and structures. The company has successfully "hard-coded" their performance environment of highly motivated, empowered employees into their business operating system. They have systematically ingrained the belief that when employees feel a certain way, they will achieve results. This focus on business outcomes combined with "the heart" (i.e., "feelings with a purpose") has sparked sustainable results year after year.

No Blanket Solution

Let's say you have a team of people reporting to you and you want to achieve the type of results that CTFS is achieving. Will you succeed by trying to create all five feelings in every one of the people who reports to you? The answer is "no." Why not?

Every person has their own unique set of emotional needs. For instance, when I feel I'm *valued* and *inspired* it produces large amounts of juice in me. I have the energy to go for hundreds of miles through all kinds of obstacles. But let my tank run dry of those two things and I have no juice to do anything of significance, even if you're filling me to the brim with the feelings of *clarity* and *support*.

The following diagnostic gives you an opportunity to discover what your top two drivers are.

What Juices You?

Check off the eleven statements you would most like to feel in your ideal work environment.

❏ I feel effective – my role is a great match for my talents
❏ I feel aligned – I'm doing what I love to do
❏ I feel I belong here – I fit in well with my team
❏ I feel secure – I'm physically, emotionally, and spiritually safe

❏ I know exactly what outcomes my manager expects of me
❏ I understand the big picture and how I contribute to it
❏ I'm clear on how my manager feels about my progress
❏ I understand and feel understood by those around me

❏ I feel equipped – I have all the tools, systems, and training I need to succeed
❏ I feel supported – my manager goes to bat for me when I need it
❏ I feel I have the freedom and authority to do what I'm responsible to do
❏ I feel that great challenges and growth opportunities are being created for me

❏ I feel people are interested in me as a person – not as a tool or an asset
❏ I feel recognized and appreciated for the contribution I make
❏ I feel I'm being treated fairly
❏ I feel my leaders listen to me in a way that makes me feel understood

❏ My work has a sense of purpose – our organization makes a difference
❏ I feel a sense of achievement – I'm held accountable for great results
❏ My manager and my leaders are authentic – they consistently walk the talk
❏ I am surrounded by people of passion and excellence

Once you've checked off the eleven feelings you would most like to feel in your ideal work situation, identify the two sections that have the most check marks beside them. These are your top two drivers – the core emotions that must be met for you to feel energized in your job.

Just as every engine needs its own unique fuel, every person requires specific feelings to energize them. It is possible to pour jet fuel into your lawn mower, but after it goes like stink for a short period of time, the engine is going to blow up. Don't assume that indiscriminately pouring feelings into people will energize them. Below, we will discuss how to identify what each person's unique energy mix is. Doing so will enable you to energize them and help them offer their discretionary effort. As the following story illustrates, if you don't learn how to do this, you could inadvertently make a costly blunder.

Buckingham and Coffman tell the story in their book *First, Break All the Rules* of John F., a manager of insurance agents who made a big mistake by failing to recognize what juiced one of his best employees, Mark D., a repeat winner of the Agent of the Year award. Mark let it be known that he hated the banal plaques that accompanied the award. He made it abundantly clear that he would prefer to be recognized by something other than a plaque.

> At the awards banquet, John announced Mark as the winner yet again, ushered him up onto the stage, and proudly presented him with his plaque. Mark took one look at it, turned to the audience, made an obscene gesture, and stalked off the stage, vowing to leave the company. The banquet was a disaster.

The story goes on to tell of John's frantic attempts to redeem himself and persuade Mark not to leave the company. John learned from Mark's colleagues that whenever Mark conversed about life outside of work, all he wanted to talk about were his two daughters and his experiences with them. He and his wife thought they could never have children, so these two little girls were his life.

John called Mark's wife and explained his dilemma.

Her inspired idea was to take a photo of the girls and mount it in a frame embossed with Mark's plaque. As the authors tell it:

> Two weeks later John held a luncheon. In front of all his agents and guests of honor, Mark's wife and daughters, John unveiled the portrait and presented it to Mark. The same prima donna who had flipped off the crowd now started to cry. Mark's trigger was his two daughters.

Mark's energy mix was, *I'm Valued* and *I'm Inspired*, but he primarily wanted to be valued and recognized as a great dad: achieving results in the area of fatherhood was what inspired him more than anything else. Any leader managing Mark could release large levels of intelligent energy inside him by focusing on his success as a dad and making sure nothing got in the way of it.

Five Crucial Conversations

There are five simple but crucial conversations your managers need to excel at if you want to release intelligent energy in your company:

1 Find the **Fit**.
2 Create **Clarity**.
3 **Support** to Success.
4 Make people Feel **Valued**.
5 Make people Feel **Inspired**.

We give managers and leaders a tool to help them conduct these conversations in a simple,systematic way. It's called the Juice Check.

Juice Check

As we said earlier, the one thing that great managers and leaders do to determine their employees' core emotional drivers is *they ask*. With a little practice, you can gain comfort using the tool on page 188. Take twenty to thirty minutes with an employee and frame the conversation as follows:

"As your manager, there is one thing that is very important to me – that you feel energized by your work. When you do, it's good for you, good for me, and good for the company. If it's OK with you, I'd like to find out the things about your work environment that make you feel energized and the things that deplete your energy. Would that be OK with you?"

If they say yes, you can continue.

"This is called a Juice Check. I'd like you to check off a green, yellow, or red box beside each question. Check off the green if you feel like you're good to *go* and fully energized on that issue – for example, if the components of your job are a great match for your talents. Check off the yellow if you feel like your energy is being drained by that issue. Check off the red if that issue is making you feel completely depleted of energy.

"Wherever you have a yellow or red check mark, I'd like to find out if there is a way for me or the rest of the team to do something that would move you more toward the green."

Engagement Is a Shared Load

Even though we are saying that it is the manager's job to ensure that employees' core emotional needs are met, it is important that managers clearly realize that they are not to try to meet those needs single-handedly. Some needs should be met by the team ("I feel understood by those around me"), other needs should be met by the organizational system, ("I feel equipped with all the resources I need to succeed"), and other needs should be met by the manager. ("My manager has my back.")

Once the person has filled out their Juice Check, ask them, "Can you share with me what you checked off for each issue? If you are green, I'd love to know why you are green and if you are yellow or red I'd love to know what it would take to move you toward the green. I'm not promising you I can move you into the green, but I want to understand what it would take. Would it be OK if I take notes to help me remember any actions I need to take?"

(For a primer on how to do a Juice Check, visit our website at www.juiceinc.ca/juicecheck.)

Team Juice Check

We have seen significant results by helping organizations learn how to conduct a Juice Check in a team format. The Team Juice Check is very similar to the individual Juice Check but is conducted in the format of a team meeting. To do it effectively, however, you will need to provide context and careful framing to your team about what it is about and what it is not about. If you are interested in using the Team Juice Check, email me at brady-wilson@juiceinc.ca or give us a call at 1-519-822-5479.

Juice Check

"My goal is to help you feel energized by your work"

	JUICED DRAINING DEPLETED	Action Required

Energized by *Fit*

Are the components of your job a match for your talents?		
Are the components of your job a match for your interests?		
Do you feel a sense of social belonging and inclusion in your team?		
Do you feel safe in your current role – psychologically and emotionally?		

Energized by *Clarity*

Do you feel clear on the expectations I have of you?		
Do you feel clear on the big picture and how you contribute to it?		
Are you clear on how your manager feels about your progress?		
Do you and your teammates understand each other?		

Energized by *Support*

Are you equipped with all the resources you need to succeed?		
Do you feel your manager "has your back" and goes to bat for you when you need it?		
Do you have the freedom and authority to do what you're responsible to do?		
Are you getting the growth opportunities and challenges that are important to you?		

Energized by *Value*

Do you feel valued as a person – not as a tool or an asset?		
Do you feel recognized and appreciated for your contribution?		
Do you feel you are being treated fairly?		
Do your leaders listen to you in a way that makes you feel completely understood?		

Energized by *Inspiration*

Do you feel inspired by the purpose of your organization?		
Are you achieving the results you want to achieve?		
Do you feel your colleagues and leaders walk the talk?		
Does the passion of your colleagues inspire you to drive for more aggressive goals?		

Discovering People's Energy Mix

You won't always be able to take every person you work with through the Juice Check. And very few people will come up to you and say, "I need you to make me feel valued right now," or, "Could I ask you for some inspiration, please?" So how do you discover what feelings energize another person if you can't do a Juice Check? Here's where you can use Pull Conversation to step into your employees' worlds and watch for the four clues that will lead you to their emotional drivers.

1 **What energizes this person's nonverbals?**
2 **What will this person make sacrifices for?**
3 **What does this person fear losing or not getting?**
4 **What "fuel" does this person pour into you?**

1 What Energizes This Person's Nonverbals?

Notice the things that make people animated in their body language and ask yourself, "What is the feeling that produced that?" I have learned that there are several nonverbal cues I can look for to tip me off on how my friend Crista is feeling about the meaning of her work. Her eyes light up, her hands start moving faster as she speaks, and her body movements are marked with certainty and confidence. Noticing what energizes her nonverbals helps me get a read on how full her tank is with inspiration, one of her primary emotional drivers.

Watching for languid body language can be instructive, too. Terry begins to slowly rub his face and forehead when his circumstances start to become unclear. You can almost see a cloud settle over his head. When I see this, I realize he will require more *clarity* to feel energized.

With practice you will begin to discover the nonverbal cues connected to the emotional drivers of the people you live and work with. Once you identify those cues, you can find ways to give them the feelings they need.

2 What Will This Person Make Sacrifices For?

Watch what people *do first*. Notice the things they will *be late for*. Discover what they'll pay *extra money for*. Listen to what they'll take pains to *make clear to others*. Connected to each of their sacrifices, you will find an emotional driver need that fuels them.

- Will they sacrifice time in a meeting to ask for the clarity they need?
- Will they sacrifice their own personal needs to be valued and accepted by their peers?
- Will they sacrifice security to have the inspiration they need?
- Will they sacrifice freedom to have the support they need?

After you have identified the things a person will make sacrifices for, find ways to help them get those feeling needs met. For example, if someone will sacrifice their own needs to be valued and accepted by their peers, their tank could be low on feeling valued. What can you do to ensure that their contribution is recognized? Is there something that is obscuring their efforts from being noticed? Do what you can to make sure they get the recognition they deserve.

3 What Does This Person Fear Losing or Not Getting?

Paul was livid when he found out that he had not been consulted about how his employees should be rewarded at the company picnic. Although he is fine with ambiguity, he desperately needs to feel that his opinion is respected and valued. When he was given no input, it triggered the fear of losing value and respect.

Notice what a person will protect at any cost. What triggers them, making them react most violently and most quickly? You will find, connected to these things, an emotional driver that is part of their Energy Mix.

When emotions like fear and anger manifest themselves, treat them as valuable dashboard gauges.

When emotions like fear and anger manifest themselves, treat them as valuable dashboard gauges. These emotions flare up to protect what the person is fearful of losing or not getting. If you react in kind and fail to understand these signals, you will miss *what's important* to this person: what their core feeling needs are. You will essentially cut yourself off from the rich data that would enable you to create value in this relationship.

The word *emotion* literally means "to move out." Emotions *move* our internal states *out* to the visible extremities of our being, broadcasting our internal needs through our faces, hands, and bodies. Remember, emotions render a vocabulary to people's most pressing inner needs.

Watch for and listen to the emotions that are being broadcast. Every one of them has a string attached to it that will lead you into an inner reality. That inner reality will tell you what is most important to the individual. Do a good job of understanding their expressed emotions and you'll find out the feeling needs that juice them.

> *Do a good job of understanding their expressed emotions and you'll find out the feeling needs that juice them.*

4 What "Fuel" Does This Person Pour into You?

People tend to assume that what's most important to them will be important to others. I love this tendency. It shows me in short order what other people's feeling needs are. If someone goes out of their way to make you feel included or to help you, they may be signaling vital clues to their own needs to feel valued and supported.

Kim, for instance, is a supervisor who consistently goes the extra mile to make people feel included. When Sheila is hired and arrives for her first day, Kim makes sure there is a beautiful fruit basket and card waiting on her desk. She takes the time for a lengthy introduction tour and makes up a schedule that guarantees that someone will be taking Sheila out for lunch every day for her first week.

If you are managing Kim, step into her world and pay close attention to how she pours the *I fit* feeling into her employees. That will probably be a strong indication of the effort you need to apply in making her feel that she is a fit with her peer supervisors.

What Are We Really Saying Here?

- People's behaviors can best be understood as an attempt to get their core emotional needs met.
- There are Five Drivers of Engagement that matter more to employees than anything else: I Fit, I'm Clear, I'm Supported, I'm Valued, and I'm Inspired.
- When employees feel these emotions at work, it releases intelligent energy in them and they become highly engaged, highly productive, highly effective, highly change-adaptive, and high performing. In short, they are able to offer their best stuff.
- This makes your job as a manager a lot easier.
- Your primary role as a manager or leader is to create an environment where your employees' five core emotional needs can be met.
- Great managers ask their employees what it would take to make them feel completely energized at work.
- The Juice Check is a simple systematic tool that enables managers to get a quick read on the energy level of an employee or a team and to identify exactly what needs to be done to energize them.

Want to Make This Happen?

- Book time with each of your direct reports and take them through the Juice Check.
- Begin to use the Juice Check on a bimonthly basis with your team.

Juice at Home

Filling Emotional Tanks

When my wife, Theresa, and I got married, someone gave us a gift that changed our lives and the futures of our (then unborn) children. It was a book by Ross Campbell called *How to Really Love Your*

Child. The simple premise of the book was that every child has an emotional tank. When their tank is full they tend to behave well. When it is empty, they tend to behave badly. It went on to teach how to fill your child's emotional tank using skills such as eye contact, physical contact, focused attention, and appropriate discipline.

We've enjoyed the results of filling our kids' emotional tanks for the past twenty-four years and have witnessed firsthand the great fruit that this produced in them. How do the five core emotional needs apply to your children?

Here's a Juice Check that's designed to help you understand what's most important to each of your children. As you go through this diagnostic, use the power of your mind's eye to imagine what they feel about each of the following statements. If your child is old enough, engage them in an informal conversation and ask them how they feel about these things. Frame each statement in the language that is appropriate for your child. Once you feel you understand where your child's tank needs to be filled up, begin to intentionally and consistently give them the feelings that they need to feel completely energized. Note: For ease and clarity, we are going to use female gender throughout this diagnostic.

I Fit

Does your child feel:
Unconditionally accepted for who she is?
Unconditionally loved without having to perform for it?
She belongs in this family?
Safe – emotionally, spiritually, and physically?

I'm Clear

Does your child feel:
Clear about your expectations of her?
Clear about how your family operates and her part in it?
Clear on how you feel about her growth and progress?
Understood by her family (i.e., she is experiencing no
     unnecessary friction due to misunderstanding)?

I'm Supported

Does your child feel:

Equipped with all the resources she needs to succeed?

That you have her back and are there to support her
when others give her a rough time?

You create growth opportunities for her, encourage her,
and take interest in her activities?

You give her a healthy amount of freedom?

I'm Valued

Does your child feel:

You relate to her and take interest in her as a person,
not just a child?

You recognize and praise her accomplishments in specific,
meaningful ways?

Fairly treated by you and her siblings?

You listen to her in a way that makes her feel her point
of view is valued and understood?

I'm Inspired

Does your child feel:

That her life has purpose?

That you hold her accountable to achieve her full potential?

That you walk the talk – modeling the things you tell her
to do?

That your excellence and the excellence of her siblings
inspire her to do her best?

Juice Your Relationships

Repairing Broken Connections

*Y*OU'VE seen how to put Pull Conversation to work in the areas of releasing intelligent energy and pulling out the Bigger Reality. But what if you have an important relationship that is severely stuck? Let's explore how Pull Conversation can help you transform a fractured or unproductive relationship.

Meeting Emotional Needs

Tanya is a shipping supervisor I know who works for Blue Sky Distribution. Although Blue Sky's sales were good, their profits were leaking out due to a significant credits-and-returns problem, an issue that stemmed largely from inaccuracy in the picking process. At the root of the inaccuracy problem was a rivalry between the receiving and shipping departments that had destroyed collaboration and trust.

Tanya got hooked on the concept of doing Pull Conversation with her employees. She decided to take her new skills out for a spin to see what they could do in the most toxic area of the organization, the "smoke pit." Blue Sky's smoke pit served as a zone of discontent where employees hung out and complained bitterly about supervisors and managers.

Tanya ventured out to this area and began asking people if there were ways that shippers and receivers could help each other. She was a well-respected supervisor and people could tell she was doing her level best to understand their issues. As she began to pull out the employees' reality, a couple of the receivers started challenging her about something her employees were doing that really bothered them.

"Your pickers go into the freezer, move stuff around, get what they need, and walk out without cleaning up after themselves. We end up having to freeze our buns off for the first hour of our shift cleaning up your mess."

To her credit, Tanya did not become defensive. Instead, she turned toward these receivers, stepped into their world, and saw their reality. She began to reflect back to them what she was hearing.

"So you've had to go into the freezer for a whole hour to clean up after us?" she said. "No wonder you guys are ticked! If we kept it clean as we used it, nobody would have to be in there for more than five minutes at a time."

The receivers began to feel more understood and valued than they had in a long time. These feelings released energy. Employees began to engage and ideas began to flow. They began to conceive of themselves as customers of each other rather than opponents of each other. They started seeing how they could help each other in simple ways.

Tanya said, "Tell you what. If I can get my pickers to clean up after themselves in the freezer, what would you guys be willing to do for us?"

"We'll make sure you have the product right at your fingertips when you need it."

"You've got a deal."

Tanya went to her team and helped them understand what keeping the freezer clean meant to the receivers and how the pickers would benefit from having product at their fingertips. Over the next several weeks, with some close oversight and encouragement, she and her team made good on their commitment.

Prior to this, pickers had to constantly ask receivers to come with a lift truck and bring things down from the high shelves, a step that resulted in a lot of waiting around and frustration. Receivers used to begrudge the fact that shippers were always interrupting them, sometimes just leaving them to wait for a while. I still remember a meeting after the smoke pit conversation when Tanya exclaimed, "We haven't had to ask the receivers to bring things down for us once this week! They've put all the product at our fingertips." In general, the number of times pickers had to go to receivers to ask them to bring stock down dropped from several times per order to once every two or three orders.

The results of this simple improvement reverberated throughout the organization as credits and returns were cut in half over a six-month period. Time and money were saved, and people felt happier and more respected in their work. Tanya's Pull Conversation in the smoke pit and her subsequent follow-up met some emotional needs inside the receivers. When their need to feel understood and valued was met, it released energy in them. The Law of Psychological Reciprocity kicked in and the receivers began to understand and appreciate the needs of the shippers.

With both shippers and receivers turning toward each other and stepping into each other's worlds, a Bigger Reality emerged: "We are one team, not two, with a common purpose, not two differing purposes." Yes, this sounds self-evident, but when two warring groups see this reality for the first time, it is a Bigger Reality that changes their behaviors significantly.

> *"We are one team, not two, with a common purpose, not two differing purposes."*

Receivers saw that their ultimate purpose was not to get product up on the shelves. Rather, it was to get the right product to the right customer at the right time. They could fulfill this overall purpose by making sure the product was where the shippers needed it, when they needed it.

Shippers could fulfill this overall purpose by keeping the freezer clean throughout the day, which made the receivers feel valued and respected. These two teams began to meet each others' emotional needs and transformed their relationship.

What is it that happens to people in Pull Conversation that triggers the release of intelligent energy? Simple. Their emotional needs get met. And when emotional needs get met, relationships become much easier to manage.

What Breaks Relationships?

Differences – or, more accurately, our inability to reconcile and harmonize our differences – are the typical cause of relational breakdown. My cultural background causes me to value things that you don't value. My family of origin has ingrained rules in me that simply have no meaning for you. My gender has inclined me to relate in certain ways that you find awkward. My age causes me to value things that your age group does not value. My personality is exactly the type that clashes with yours.

Enrico, a dashing twenty-five-year-old from Brazil, is a colleague of forty-five-year-old Janet, who is from the United States. They work together on a sales team in a Chicago ad agency.

Enrico has a very elastic view of time: it stretches to accommodate him. Where he's from, no one expects you to show up at an 8:00 A.M. meeting until 8:30 A.M. In fact, people would consider you somewhat rigid if you did.

Janet, on the other hand, has a very precise view of time. She was raised in a culture where punctuality equaled performance. On top of that, her dad took great pains to impress on her that she should never arrive late to a meeting. "It's a sign of disrespect to others," he always said.

Enrico is flamboyant, charming, and funny. Janet is reserved, organized, and proper.

You can see how things are shaping up. After their first "incident" with a client, where Enrico appeared at the meeting twenty minutes late, Janet approached him quite forcefully.

"I was completely mortified by your performance," she said. "I need to count on you to never do that again."

"I don't understand," Enrico said. "They loved me. Didn't you see those guys light up when I started to talk about our new concept? I saved that meeting."

"I'm not talking about that. I'm talking about the fact that you showed up late. That sort of thing is simply not acceptable to me, or to the client."

"I think you're a little uptight. I joked with them a little about being on Brazilian time. They loved it."

You can see where this is going to end up in a month's time. The inability to reconcile the differences in culture, family of origin, gender, age, and personality is going to produce a complete relational meltdown.

Our differences instantly cause tension. And energy will always emerge out of relational tension. The question is, are you capable of pulling out intelligent energy from the tension, or will destructive energy emerge?

It's your ability to become adept at Pull Conversation that's going to determine the outcome. What do you suppose the chances are that you will get the assistance of the other person in resolving this situation?

How Push Fouls Up Relationships

Think of ten people that you are in relationship with. Our research demonstrates that when you relate to these ten people, six of them will push, three of them will acquiesce, and only one of them will pull.

This means that in any one of your relationships, there is a 66% chance that the other person is taking a push approach with you. That's six out of ten people. And unless you are an exceptional communicator, there's a 66% chance that you are taking a push approach with others.

Pushing can be very problematic for relationships, for three main reasons.

1 A push approach fails to harmonize differences.
2 A push approach causes you to misread other people's motives.
3 A push approach causes you to misperceive the appropriate action to take to repair the relationship.

Failing to Harmonize Differences

As this book has argued, getting to the Bigger Reality enables us to go far beyond tolerating one another. It enables us to harmonize our differences and thrive together. In a stuck situation, the Bigger Reality that often unlocks intelligent energy is, "We are one."

Push, however, locks us into a stance where you are my opponent, my enemy, my competitor. There is very little chance, if we take this stance, that we will harmonize our differences.

Misreading Other People's Motives

When you don't take the time to pull out the other person's point of view, you are left with only your own perceptions with which to build reality. People stuck in this position have a tendency to perceive others through their own motivational value system (the way they see the world).

For example, when I see my friend demonstrate his anger, and I fail to pull out his reality, I believe that he is at a 9.5 on the rage scale. After all, that's where I'd have to be to act like that. Because I believe he is very angry, I respond accordingly. There's a problem with this style of relating: the chances of being accurate when you interpret others' words and actions through your motivational value system are very slim, about as slim as your fingerprints or retinas being an exact match. Why?

Other people are different from you. You are pretty much guaranteed to experience misunderstanding, suspicion, and mistrust until you learn to interpret others' words and actions through their motivational value system rather than your own. Most often, their style is not right or wrong, it's just different from yours.

Transforming relationships is largely a matter of reconciling your differences with others by learning to step into their world, pull out their reality, and interpret their words and actions through their motivational value system. When you learn to do this, you can avoid offending others. But even if you do happen to offend, you can clean up the hurt and misunderstanding in a productive way and move on with the relationship.

Misperceiving the Appropriate Action to Take

Think of a time when someone did or said something that deeply hurt you. Later they came to you and offered a perfunctory "sorry." Not wanting to be bitter, you did your best to forgive the person, but the slightest provocation on their part still triggered a reaction in you, indicating that your heart was still festering and unhealed. It seemed that no matter how hard you tried to forgive, there was a big sliver stuck in your heart that just couldn't be dislodged.

If you're fortunate, that person will step into your world and feel the true extent of your hurt. When they do that, they will realize that their first apology was trivial compared with the pain they inflicted on you.

Seeing how they have hurt you, they can now offer an apology with understanding and empathy. "I am so sorry for how I hurt you. Now I see the implications of my actions and why my words were so painful for you. Please forgive me."

This apology – commensurate with the intensity of the pain – releases true forgiveness inside you and pulls the sliver of bitterness from your heart. Best of all, there's nothing to trigger the reactions.

You never really know the appropriate action to take to repair a relationship until you see the size of the offense from the other person's point of view.

Repairing Relationships

Repairing a Threatened Relationship

About ten years ago, I was experiencing a lot of misunderstanding and friction in my relationship with my boss, Bob. In spite of many attempts to talk things through, our relationship had deteriorated to the point where we no longer had any desire to work together. The twisted irony of the whole situation was that I trained people to understand one another but was mired in a seemingly intractable misunderstanding myself.

To step into Bob's world, I had to *get past my self*: I had fears ("I'll be misunderstood"), assumptions ("He wants to get rid of me"), defensiveness ("I know I'm right about this issue and he has to see this"), and judgments ("He's against me, not for me").

To get past my self I had to come to the point where I firmly believed that the reward would be worth the pain. When I came to that place, I approached Bob. I admitted that I was fearful that I might be misunderstood but that I wanted to let him look inside some of my assumptions. I gave him a sheet of paper entitled, "Assumptions I have about how Bob sees me." On the list were such things as, "I assume that Bob sees me as trying to take over his position" and "I assume that Bob thinks I'm criticizing him behind his back."

Next, with the help of a friend to facilitate the dialogue, Bob and I embarked on a process to discover which of our assumptions about each other were off the wall and which ones were accurate. To inquire deeply into Bob's frame of reference, I had to really want to understand his feelings, beliefs, and judgments. As he described situations that had been injurious to him, I *pictured in my mind's eye what it was like to be him in this situation.* Then I clarified the things I heard and *reflected back* Bob's feelings. Demonstrating that I understood his true intentions helped him feel understood by me.

He, in turn, worked hard to understand where I was coming from. Ultimately, the core emotional needs we were both missing were met through the process. This energized the relationship and repaired the bridge of trust that had broken down between us.

Ten years later, Bob and I still work together occasionally and enjoy our relationship. I discovered at a deep level that he really was *for* me and he discovered I wasn't trying to take anything away from him. The uncanny thing is, having passed through each other's worlds, we who were polar opposites have become more like each other, and in ways that have made both of us more mature.

There are at least two things we can learn from this story. First, there can be great benefit in pulling in a neutral facilitator to help you get to a Bigger Reality. Often we assume it's not OK to get others involved, but no such rule has ever been written. Second, it can be very helpful to make your assumptions explicit, even writing them down for the other person to verify or clarify.

In the situation above, Bob and I were both willing to change. But what happens when one person has a deeply ingrained set of toxic habits? Can such a relationship be transformed? Thankfully, even the most entrenched habits can be changed. It does, however, require significant time and commitment.

Repairing Toxic Relationships

Several years ago, I was brought in to do a major training and coaching intervention in a manufacturing organization. The machine shop was a short-circuited environment. Negative energy was sparking all over. Ned, the shop manager, was an ex-marine who was given to fits of rage. When he got angry he would throw hunks of metal around the machine shop. The workers were tough men but Ned made all of them cringe.

Dan, the shop foreman, also had an anger problem that manifested itself in seething, public putdowns. Dan had been involved in a forklift incident where an employee had almost been killed. Fear filled the environment. Employees did not trust or respect management in general, nor would they offer them anything beyond the bare minimum of information and effort.

Despite the precision work that they were expected to do turning out micro-tuned high-strength steel rods, workers on the shop floor knew they couldn't go to either Ned or Dan if there was a problem. They'd either be ignored, partronized, or called idiots to their faces.

Not surprisingly, workers were hiding their scrap to cover up any evidence of mistakes. When engineers made errors in their plans, the workers, rather than pushing things back up through the system for correction and risking a scene, would try to figure out how to compensate for the mistake themselves, making their own changes to the drawings. Not only were the engineers not learning from their mistakes, the machinists were wasting scrap as they figured things out.

The plant manager wasn't taking action, but the Business Unit Manager and HR manager finally had enough. They were willing to do whatever it took to get things turned around.

Of course, it wasn't the shop floor at all that needed to change. It was the people and their relationships. Over a five-month period, Ned and Dan and the entire company were taken through an intensive – and sometimes painful – training/coaching course on how to do dialogue. All of it was focused on creating a shared understanding of a Bigger Reality between the managers and the workers. And every single dialogue experience began with agreements about respect.

Over time, as Ned, Dan, and other managers learned how to step into the worlds of their employees, they began to see and feel the reality of all the anxieties, fears, and pain that their staff had been living with. They were disturbed by what they heard – and shocked that they had been totally deaf to it before. Feeling the realities of his machine-shop employees made an imprint on Ned. He began to demonstrate more respect for his men. As they began to feel respected, their levels of engagement rose, which began to have an impact on the machine shop's results.

A year later, to find out if Ned had really turned the corner, I talked to someone in the shop who held no fondness for him. He told me, "Ned's a changed man all right." It is not common for me to see a man near retirement making a lasting change, but such is the power of seeing and feeling the pain you have caused others. The see – feel – change sequence showed up powerfully here. And the bonus was that Dan underwent a similar change.

Two years later, the Business Unit Manager wrote me and documented the results of what had become a juiced environment:

- The team has led the division in profitability for the last two years and remains well ahead of other business units they deal with. "We are clearly the most profitable competitor in our industry."
- Even in the midst of some major organizational changes and the reforming of the company, the unit "continues to meet elevated expectations and challenges itself to do more."

- A recent customer survey gave the unit very high marks for quality and for the support provided in all areas of technology and service.
- All previous records on safety have been broken, with the unit exceeding 550 days without a lost-time accident.

I am coming to believe that conversation can change anyone if enough inquiry and directness are applied. But as the following story illustrates, the need for inquiry and directness becomes even more critical when you are facing language barriers.

"American Capitalist Pig Go Home"

This was the message that welcomed Robert Widham (his real name) when he arrived in France to turn around Stanley Works' stormy French subsidiary. The plant had been overtaken by communist unions that wanted nothing more than for Widham to turn tail and return, defeated, to the U.S.

Widham approached this thorny relationship issue the same way he had approached other crises throughout his career: by being direct, working hard, and stepping into his opponents' worlds.

His first step was, for many leaders, an uncommon one. When the union reps were brought in, Widham said, "Look, I don't understand your language or your culture, would you give me a month?"

Luckily, they agreed. On top of his demanding schedule as new managing director of a turbulent plant, Widham began the arduous task of learning a new language.

"I spent about four hours every night learning French," he said, "and after two weeks I wouldn't let anybody speak to me in English at all. And within four weeks I was able to have a working knowledge of French."

Why not hire a simultaneous interpreter? Why not get a bilingual team member to translate for him? Why waste four hours a night and risk insulting the French by butchering their beloved tongue? Why risk unnecessary misunderstandings by undertaking highly charged, complex conversations in an unfamiliar language?

Because he believed that empathy had the power to unlock the most intractable situation. And that empathy meant stepping into their world to learn and speak their language. But would all this be enough to prevail in this situation?

Widham had to achieve two seemingly opposing goals simultaneously: win the trust of the workers and engineer a head-on collision with the unions. He began developing a strong connection with his workers by holding face-to-face communication meetings (inquiry) and sponsoring sporting days. He confronted the unions by suing them for defamation of character (directness) after they put up posters portraying him and his managers as robbers. In the final analysis, the union offered an apology and told Widham they would stop attacking his managers but would continue to attack him – a proposition that suited him fine.

Within four years, the plant was one of Stanley's top performers and Widham was promoted back to the home office.

The Miracle of Peace

Molly and Arthur Rouner are on the mission of their lives: they're out to build peace in Rwanda. The mass genocide of a decade ago produced a challenge that would severely test the capability of conversation to transform relationships. When two cultures clash in acts of hatred and twisted violence, the wounds within individuals and throughout the country are profound. Why would a couple from the American midwest want to spend their retirement years traveling to this country several times a year and dealing with such deep pain? Who could imagine that they could make a difference in such devastation?

And yet they *are* making a difference, small group by small group, as they host meetings for Hutus and Tutsis to come together and talk about their experiences.

According to the Rouners, "Survivors of genocide bear deep wounds, often physically, emotionally, and spiritually."

They point out that while many outsiders have come to Rwanda and Burundi to help through seminars and workshops, lectures, and teaching on reconciliation, the cry from many who have been to these seminars is, "But how can we do these things we've been taught when we still have so much wounding and pain inside us?"

The Rouners' approach is different: they don't teach, they "go to the places of killing in Rwanda and Burundi, to sit with the people there, loving them and listening to their hurts ..."

People talk and listen to one another. It's as simple and as profound as that. Through this open space of true dialogue, miracles happen. People's hurts begin to be healed; they begin to see ways in which they can reconcile with others; and they begin to have a dream for their future and the future of Rwanda.

Two pastors, one a Hutu and the other a Tutsi, attended such a meeting and became friends. They realized that they could work together – that they *needed* to work together, for their own healing and to show Rwandans that there is hope for reconciliation. They describe their experience in the video *Lasting Peace*, produced by the Pilgrim Center for Reconciliation.

> Jean-Baptiste: *Most Rwandans are still bearing the marks of the genocide. Everywhere I meet people who have the marks of the machete, and others remember how they escaped miraculously, and the wounds are still fresh.*
>
> Philippe: *And then people saw us together. When we went somewhere where people could not eat together, work together, sleep together, we shared our testimony, and we shared how we love one another. People wondered, and they came, and they cried. They would say, "We believe that reconciliation is possible, because of you two, a Hutu and a Tutsi, working together."*
>
> Jean-Baptiste: *There is a risk of being hated by my own people, my own family, because I could seem as a betrayer if I saw good things towards the Tutsis ... But when I see someone who is totally healed, even one, I say, "This is a miracle and I want to fight for this until Rwandans experience this healing process."*
>
> Philippe: *Actually, it is a process that I have experienced: you step forward until you get healed ... totally. I am healed totally.*

This story takes the see – feel – change sequence to a whole new level. When onlookers saw these two men together and felt the impact of their unity, it changed them. They have not only found peace, they are a living, walking picture of peace that is transforming the people around them. 1+1 = 5. A miracle indeed!

A Word on Forgiveness

It is virtually impossible to transform broken relationships without the mending force of forgiveness. One may argue, "Forgiveness doesn't belong in business. It's a religious word." My opinion is that forgiveness is a relational word, not a religious word, and it is a crucial element in removing the toxic seepage of bitterness and

Forgiveness is a relational word, not a religious word, and it is a crucial element in removing the toxic seepage of bitterness and resentment.

resentment that can destroy trust and collaboration in the workplace. If you have any long-term relationship that is worth anything, you have probably had to exercise the discipline of forgiveness to sustain that relationship.

Forgiveness is very simple to understand and very difficult to do. When you forgive someone, you choose not to hold their offense against them. It is, however, important to note that forgiveness does *not* mean that:

- You condone their action.
- You're saying it was OK for them to hurt you.
- You will allow them to continue to run roughshod over you.

It simply means that you choose not to hold their offense against them. This, of course, requires true maturity.

Mont Fleur: Intelligent Energy Changes a Country

Africa is also the setting of our second story of widespread relational transformation, this one recounting the beginnings of the turnaround in South Africa.

How much energy can you generate with authentic, pulling conversation?

In the early 1990s, South Africa was hopelessly mired in an intractable social and political dilemma. Despite Nelson Mandela's miraculous release from prison by F.W de Klerk, the country seemed impossibly torn and unmendable.

In 1991, Adam Kahane, a Canadian working for Shell and living in the UK, was invited to facilitate a scenario planning/dialogue project for the black left-wing opposition and its white group of adversaries. He tells the story in his book, *Solving Tough Problems.*

> The essence of the Mont Fleur process, I saw, was that a small group of deeply committed leaders, representing a cross-section of a society that the world considered irretrievably stuck, had sat down together to talk broadly and profoundly about what was going on and what should be done.

The workshops were facilitated at Mont Fleur Conference Center outside Capetown. Kahane describes his early view of the process:

> I could see that this scenario meeting was not going to be like the Shell ones I was used to. We were not working on an ordinary problem of organizational strategy but on an extraordinary national transformation.

Kahane worked with this devoted group over several months, creating scenarios of what the future of South Africa could be. Four scenarios were finally chosen, three negative and one positive. Now the conversation needed to go public. The scenarios were shared abroad on a national scale. A booklet was inserted into a leading paper and the scenarios were even turned into a cartoon video.

> Most importantly, they ran more than 100 workshops for leadership groups of their own and other influential political, business and civic organizations, where the four scenarios were presented and debated.

The "national conversation" sparked by the four scenarios and the dialogue in the workshops began to evoke a sense of collaborative energy among South Africa's leaders. This became the active ingredient that drove the success of the country's turnaround in the 1990s.

What Are We Really Saying Here?

- Differences are guaranteed in relationships.
- Differences create tension.

- Your ability to harmonize your differences is the key to pulling intelligent energy out of the tension.
- It's the intelligent energy that transforms the relationship.
- Transforming relationships is a *see – feel – change* process. You help someone see and feel a different reality. This enables them to change.
- You never really know the appropriate action to take to repair a relationship until you see the size of the offense from the other person's point of view.

Want to Make This Happen?

- Do you have one relationship that needs to be reconciled but appears to be beyond hope of reconciliation? If a Hutu–Tutsi relationship can be healed, then there's a chance that your relationship can be healed, too.
- Ask the individual if they would be willing to work together on rebuilding the relationship. If they are game, start the process by stepping into their world and seeking to understand their reality concerning how you have caused them injury. Avoid the temptation to defend yourself, justify your actions, psychoanalyze them, or even agree with them. At this point, your mission is simply to see and feel their reality and to reflect it back so they feel assured you understand them.
- Once you have demonstrated your understanding, ask them to do for you what you have done for them. When you have understood each other as well as you can, offer each other an apology that is commensurate with the hurt that you have caused, then forgive each other – choosing to not hold the grievance against each other as you move forward in the relationship.
- This paves the way for you to discover a Bigger Reality that will enable the relationship to move forward.

Juice at Home

Lost in a Supermarket

The movie *Stepmom* is a great story of a transformed relationship.

Jackie is a mom who is dying of cancer. She is separated from her former husband, Luke. Isabel is the pretty new girlfriend who has stolen Luke's heart away.

Isabel makes a big mistake at the beginning of the movie, losing Jackie's five-year-old son, Ben, in a crowd. Jackie will not let her live it down.

But over time, Jackie has come to "get" that Isabel really loves her kids and is committed to caring for them for the long haul. She invites Julia to a restaurant where she confesses that she also lost Ben once, in a supermarket.

"That's impossible," Isabel says. "You could never leave that kid for one second."

Isabel goes on to admit that she never wanted to be a mom. "Well, sharing it with you is one thing – carrying it alone the rest of my life ... always being compared to you. You're perfect. They worship you."

"What do I have that you don't?" Jackie asks her.

Isabel makes quite a speech in response. "You know every story, every wound, every memory. Their whole life's happiness is wrapped up ... in ... you ... Look down the road at her wedding. I'm in a room ... alone with her ... fitting her veil ... fluffing her dress ... telling her no woman has ever looked as beautiful. And my fear is that she'll be thinking, 'I wish my mom was here.'"

To which Jackie replies, "But the truth is ... she doesn't have to choose. She can have us both ... love us both. And she will be a better person because of me and because of you. I have their past and you can have their future."

The end of the movie shows Jackie pulling Isabel into the Christmas family picture – a clear sign that she is accepting her as the mother of the children she is about to leave behind.

"Cultural Architects to Work!"

Sixteen Ways to Produce Juice

Cultural Architects

In his book *The Unstoppable Force*, Erwin McManus refers to leaders as cultural architects. If you are a leader or manager, you have a unique ability to shape the culture within your sphere of influence. As we wrap up this book, let's reflect back on the leaders (capital "L" and small "l") that you have met in this book and unpack the specific attitudes and actions that enabled them to release their company's intelligent energy. Pick out the pragmatic suggestions that most apply to you as you engage in being the architect of a juice-filled environment.

1 Create a Red Room

The leaders of the large Australian telecommunications company empowered Amanda to kick-start the dialogue process in their organization, providing an opportunity for their employees to converse simply within a safe, funky, creative environment. In the process they learned that *conversation releases energy*. Unit B doubled its income in six months and created a culture of joy at work. How can you implement the Red Room concept in your organization?

2 Walk the Line

Dino, the supervisor with the chanting line of workers, created a strong bond of connection with his men as he weaved back and forth through the line. Dino instinctively realized that *energy is the ability to do work*, so he spent time energizing his employees with short, personal, face-to-face conversations to find out what was going on in their lives. While other supervisors struggled with absenteeism and scrambled to get temps, Dino's men showed up regularly and moved through an amazing mountain of work every night. How will you use short, personal check-ins to release energy in your employees?

3 Step Out of Your World

David created a cultural turnaround when he did the hard work of stepping out of his world, letting go of his defensiveness and stepping into the world of his leadership team. When the Bigger Reality was uncovered, intelligent energy was released and the team started anticipating one another's needs and leveraging one another's efforts. His team began to achieve unprecedented results, doubling their growth over a twelve-month period.

It's tempting to say, "I've got no time for all this Pull Conversation stuff. It's quicker to just push!" But take note: by pulling, *David was able to achieve in two short days what he had been unable to accomplish in two years of dogged pushing.* Identify the areas where you have been pushing your reality on your team. Book an adequate chunk of time to step out of your world and into theirs. Discover the unmet emotional needs that are causing hidden resistance. Find out how to get those needs met through Pull Conversation.

4 Create a Conversation Relay

The leaders of the scooter company created an environment of fifteen-minute relay conversations. In the space of a single hour, priorities and concerns and understood were goals clarified, committed to, and communicated through the managers, directors, and VPs and right into the CEO's office. Remember, *the more power and authority you have, the harder it is to get your hands on reality.* How could you create this type of relay in your organization?

5 Pull Out Concerns

Steve learned that technological solutions are doomed to fail if they aren't steeped in face-to-face conversation. His operators dug in and refused to implement the new system. To his credit, Steve shifted the environment from push to pull, began to understand the concerns of his employees and was able to get the implementation on track. In the process, he learned that *"people almost never change without feeling understood first."* What "stuck" implementation or project do you need to get moving? Do the work of pulling out the hidden concerns, misgivings, and fears that are causing resistance and find a way to address those concerns to employees' satisfaction.

6 Find Language That Works for Them

Bill, the nuclear engineer, shifted from a push to a Pull orientation in his relationship with the Atomic Energy Commission. He pulled out their reality, discovered a way to pull them into his reality, and discovered a Bigger Reality – a solution that worked for both of them. By understanding them first, he won their trust and was able to save the company a stunning $1.2 million. Pick the one area in which it is crucial for you to influence people to change. Find a way to frame your message in a way that is easy for them to understand and buy into.

7 Uncover the Little Wins

Fred deVries created an environment with his customers that left them feeling juiced. Although Fred felt strongly that he had the right solution for this large hospital, he refrained from pushing his point of view on the decision-makers. Perhaps he knew instinctively that *people will tolerate your conclusions ... and act on their own.* He stepped into his customers' world, understood what was most important to them, and landed a $7.8 million deal – the sale of a lifetime.

Which customer's world do you need to step into more deeply? Discover what the little wins are for them and begin to make them happen.

8 Ask "What's Most Important" Questions

Rob LeBlanc asks the questions that pull out *what's important* for each prospective car buyer. Soon he understands their reality: their specific definition of value – of performance, looks, safety, maintenance, or theft protection. As he takes his customers for a test drive, Rob is able to draw their attention to the specific traits of the car that will be of most interest to them. The customer starts to feel energized about the purchase of this vehicle. Time invested in the understanding phase cuts Rob's time in half in the negotiation phase, where it's common for him to get laydowns, the full sales price of the vehicle being laid down on his desk. *Trust = Speed.*

Ask the questions that will get you to a clear understanding of what's most important to your customers.

9 Be Direct to Earn Respect

Brian took over an underperforming maintenance department and faced the spine-numbing challenge of a team mutiny. He used the directness of Pull Conversation to hold his ground and lay out in bald terms the new reality that his team could expect. By being consistent, tenacious, and fair, Brian expanded his leadership influence and released intelligent energy into his department.

Is someone not respecting you? Speak your truth productively to them in a respectful, firm, and consistent way.

10 Invest the Time to Listen

Catherine demonstrated respect. Instead of writing off the cranky and incorrigible Myrna, she decided to *look again*. As a result, she discovered that Myrna responded well when someone simply took an interest in her. Catherine got surprising results. She received her work back from Myrna, on time, mistake free, complete with creative innovations.

Who is your Myrna? Show respect to this person. Drop by their work area and demonstrate authentic interest in what's important to them. Pull out their best stuff.

11 Go Out into the Smoke Pit

Tanya ventured out to the smoke pit, pulled out the concerns of the receiving team, pulled them into her reality, and a Bigger Reality emerged: the receivers and shippers were one team, not two, with a common purpose, not two differing purposes. As people began to see and feel this reality, it changed their behaviors. Accuracy shot up in the picking area and credits and returns were cut in half over a six-month period.

What is the smoke pit in your organization, the place where all the complaining happens? Venture into it to discover what people's real concerns are. Discover what you can do to meet people's core emotional needs.

12 Embed a Mindset of "Emotions Drive Results"

Tom Gauld of Canadian Tire Financial Services systematically ingrained a belief within his leadership team that when employees feel a certain way, they will achieve significant results. This belief paid off handsomely in both hard and soft measures.

Does your leadership team believe that their fundamental task as leaders is to create an environment where your employees' core emotional needs are met? What will you do to create a see – feel – change process that will enable them to embrace this belief and behave accordingly?

13 Help the Offender Feel Others' Hurts

It has been said that most of our problems are caused by old white guys with white hair. Do you have a man between fifty and sixty years old who needs to change but is oblivious to his need? No one thought Ned was capable of change. No one thought he would ever respect his men. The power of Pull Conversation delightfully shocked us all.

Get your Ned into an intervention where he is required to see and feel the downstream implications of his actions in others' lives. One of two good things can come out of this:

- Ned will see and feel and change.
- Ned will choose not to see and feel and change and you will be able to offer him a choicepoint about his future in the organization.

14 Facilitate Reconciliation

The Rouners use their conversation skills to help injured parties reconcile to each other. Are you stuck in the middle of two individuals who can't or won't see eye to eye? As a neutral but concerned mediator, introduce the Pull Conversation model and help them through the process.

15 Hold Action-Oriented Town Halls

Kathy Bardswick used the town-hall forum to meet with her employees across the nation, hear first-hand what was going well and what needed to change. Then she made sure that action was taken as quickly as possible and got back to people so they would see and feel their suggestions being enacted. People's core emotional needs to feel supported, valued, and inspired were met through Kathy and her leadership team.

Do you ever get out of head office? I mean in a meaningful way? The ripple effect you will create in your organization if you invest the time to do what Kathy did will be astounding. But first, ensure that you and your leadership team have the corporate will to either act on what your employees say or help them understand why you can't. Interestingly enough, employees will typically be OK with whatever decision you make *if they believe* that you understand their concerns and authentically value their input.

16 Ask

Great managers ask their employees what it would take for them to feel completely energized at work. Use the Juice Check as a mechanism to have short, meaningful conversations with your employees to discover what you, the team or the organization can do to meet their core emotional needs and unlock their engagement.

What Have We Really Said in This Book?

- Conversation releases energy.
- Pull Conversation releases intelligent energy.
- Conversation is the operating system that energizes and drives every application in your organization.
- The quality of your organization is as good as the quality of the conversations of your people.
- Pull enables others to understand you more quickly and deeply.
- Pull gives you context, the ability to see as a sensible whole what others see as disconnected parts.
- When you pull someone into your world and help them see and feel your reality, you enable them to change.
- When you pull out the Bigger Reality, the smartest decisions become apparent and intelligent energy is released.
- Intelligent energy generates high-performing behaviors.
- High-performing behaviors produce sustained results.
- Therefore, Pull Conversation is the quickest route to sustained results.
- Demonstrating respect pulls out people's brilliance, their best stuff.
- When people's core emotional needs are met, it energizes them to offer their discretionary effort.
- Conversation is the instrument that is capable of creating radical relational transformations.
- Leaders are the cultural architects who have the capacity to create environments where it feels good to work and it's easier to get results.
- Leaders do this by engaging people in Pull Conversations.

Appendix

Debunking the 7%–38%–55% Communications Fallacy

*P*ERHAPS you've run into the 7%–38%–55% rule. A trainer tells you that "research has shown" that people extract 7% of their meaning from your actual words, 38% from your tone of voice, and 55% from your body language. If this was true, it would mean that a walloping 93% of people's messages are communicated through nonverbals.

There are two problems with this rule. First, it just doesn't line up with our experience. Second, it has been misapplied to become a sweeping generalization of how interpersonal communication works when in fact it is based on a small piece of research intended to demonstrate one particular point.

The research was conducted with college students in the 1960s by a UCLA professor named Albert Mehrabian. To help you understand this situation, let's transport you back in time and make you a participant in Mehrabian's research.

In the first experiment you listen to tape-recorded words and your mission is to discern if the person speaking them likes you, dislikes you, or is neutral toward you. There are nine words in total.

"Honey," "dear," and "thanks" are used to indicate liking. "Brute," "don't," and "terrible" are used to indicate disliking. "Maybe," "really," and "oh" are used to indicate neutrality.

The speaker is coached to alter his tone of voice three times as he says each set of three words. For instance, he says "honey" in a nasty tone of voice, says "dear" in a neutral tone of voice, and says "thanks" in a sweet tone of voice.

You may not be shocked to discover that the tone of the speaker's voice carries the day. In this particular setting, tone is much more influential than the meaning of the words themselves in determining your assessment of the speaker's true feelings.

Now another wrinkle is thrown into the study. You listen to the nine words spoken in the varying tones of voice, but this time you are also shown photographs with varying facial expressions as you listen to each word. Your task is to guess the speaker's true feelings based on the facial expressions, the tone of voice, and the words.

Once again, you may not be overly astonished to find that this time the facial expressions win the day.

The researchers synthesized the statistical results and arrived at the now famous rule that states that a listener's assessment of a speaker's feelings is based on the words themselves only 7% of the time; on the tone of voice 38% of the time; and on nonverbals a staggering 55% of the time.

How did this fallacy become accepted in such a wholesale fashion? I remember sharing these conclusions with audiences back in the early 1990s. People would be amazed as I unveiled the discovery that 93% of their communication was delivered through nonverbals.

I think the importance of nonverbals was a revelation to people because we had summarily ignored them to that point. This created an appetite that made these hard-to-swallow statistics quite palatable. And I'm not sure that swallowing the 7%–38%–55% fallacy created much damage in the workplace. It's healthy to be reminded of the powerful role of nonverbals in communication. My simple point is that I don't want anything to cause people to lose sight of the immense importance of their words in conveying meaning to their listeners.

A JUICE Glossary

ANALYZE. To loosen throughout, to take apart. (*ana* – throughout + *lyein* – to loosen)

ARROGANCE. Overbearing or haughty. (from *arrogantia*, the title in Roman law by which a person owned a slave)

ASSUME. To take for granted. (*ad* – to + *sumere* – to take)

COGNITION. To know together. (*co* – together + *noscere* – to know)

COGNIZANCE. To be born together. (*co* – together + *nasci* – to be born)

COHERENCE. To stick together. (*co* – together + *haerere* – to stick)

COMMUNICATION. The act of becoming one with or one together. (*com* – together + *uni* – one + *cation* – the action of)

COMPROMISE. To promise together. (*com* – together + *promittere* – to promise)

CONTEXT. To weave together. (*com* – together + *texere* – to weave)

CONVERSATION. To turn together. (*com* – together + *vertere* – to turn)

DEBATE. To beat down in order to resolve. (*de* – down + *batre* – to strike)

DIALOGUE. Meaning or reality flowing through. (*dia* – through + *logos* – reality)

DICHOTOMY. To cut in two. (*dicho* – in two + *temnein* – to cut).

DISCUSS. To shake something apart. (*dis* – apart + *quatere* – to shake)

EMOTION. To move out. (*e* – out + *movere* – to move)

EXPRESS. To press or push outwards. (*ex* – out + *pressare* – to press)

INFORM. To form within. (*informare* – to give form to)

INFORMATION. That which gives form.

INSIGHT. Seeing into.

NECESSARY. What cannot be turned aside. (*necesse* – don't yield).

RECOGNIZE. To know again. (*re* – again + *cognoscere* – to know)

REFLECT. To bend back the meaning. (*re* – back + *flectere* – to bend)

RESPECT. To look again. (*re* – again + *specere* – to look)

SUSPEND. To hang from or to hang under. (*sub* – under + *pendere* – to hang)

UNDERSTAND. To stand under. (*under* – under + *standan* – to stand) Picture two friends in a large crowd several centuries ago. The Queen is passing through town and it's impossible for either friend to see over the crowd. One friend allows the other to get up on his back and asks him to describe what is happening. As he understands (stands under) his friend, he sees the events through his friend's eyes. Seeing and feeling another's reality is understanding.

UNIFY. To join together so as to form a whole, to make one, to be merged into one, pulling that which is fragmented together. (*unus* – one + *facere* – to make)

Bibliography

Articles, Reports

Aldag, Ray and Wayne Reschke. "Employee Value Added: Measuring Discretionary Effort and Its Value to the Organization." Center for Organizational Effectiveness, 1997.

BlessingWhite. *Employee Engagment Report 2005*.

Conger, Jay A. "The Necessary Art of Persuasion." *Harvard Business Review*, May 1998.

Cooperrider, David L. "Positive Image, Positive Action: The Affirmative Basis of Organizations." In Srivasta, Suresh and David L. Cooperrider. *Appreciative Management and Leadership: The Power of Positive Thought and Action in Organizations* (rev. ed.) San Francisco: Jossey-Bass, 1990.

Corporate Leadership Council. *Driving Performance and Retention Through Employee Engagement*. Washington: Corporate Executive Board, 2004.

Corporate Leadership Council. *2002 Performance Management Survey*. Washington: Corporate Executive Board, 2002.

Davey, Liane, Nancy Gore, Owen Parker. "Reaching Productive Engagement: The Four Pillar Approach to Managing Investment in Human Capital." *Ivey Business Journal*, July–August 2003.

Hallowell, Edward M. "The Human Moment at Work." *Harvard Business Review*, Jan. 1, 1999.

Hoover, Gretchen. "Maintaining Employee Engagement When Communicating Difficult Issues." *Communication World*, Nov.–Dec. 2005.

Kandath, Krishna, John Oetzel, Everett Rogers, Ann Mayer-Guell. "Conflict in Virtual Communication." San Francisco: International Association of Business Communicators, 2005.

Kegan, Robert and Lisa Laskow Lahey. "The Real Reason People Won't Change." *Harvard Business Review*, Nov. 2001.

Kinni, Theodore. "Is One-Dimensional Communication Limiting Your Leadership?" *Harvard Business Review*, May 2003.

Kofman, Fred and Peter M. Senge. "Communities of Commitment: The Heart of Learning Organizations." In Chawla, Sarita and John Renesch (eds.). *Learning Organizations: Developing Cultures for Tomorrow's Workplace*. Portland: Productivity Press, 1995.

Mehrabian, Albert and Susan R. Ferris. "Inference of Attitudes from Non-verbal Communication in Two Channels." *Journal of Consulting Psychology* 31 (3), 1967.

Mehrabian, Albert and Morton Wiener. "Decoding of Inconsistent Communications." *Journal of Personality and Social Psychology* 6 (1), 1967.

Melcrum. *Employee Engagement: How to Build a High-Performance Workforce*. Melcrum Publishing, 2005.

Riggio, R.E. and S.J. Taylor. "Personality and Communication Skills in Predictions of Hospice Nurse Performance." *Journal of Business and Psychology*, Dec. 2000.

Rogen International. "Balancing E-mail and Face to Face in Workplace Communication." March–April 2001.

Rogers, Carl R. "A Theory of Therapy, Personality, and Interpersonal Relationships, as Developed in the Client-Centered Framework." In S. Koch (ed.). *Psychology: A Study of Science* (vol. 3). New York: McGraw-Hill, 1959.

Shaw, Kieron. "An Engagement Strategy Process for Communicators." *Strategic Communication Management*, April–May 2005.

Standish Group. *Chaos Report*. Published annually.

Towers Perrin. *Reconnecting With Employees: Quantifying the Value of Engaging Your Workforce*. 2005.

Towers Perrin. *Ten Steps to Creating an Engaged Workforce: Key European Findings*. Towers Perrin Global Workforce Study, 2005.

Towers Perrin. *Working Today: Exploring Employees' Emotional Connections to Their Jobs.* Towers Perrin/Gang & Gang, 2003.

Towers Perrin. *Working Today: Understanding What Drives Employee Engagement.* Towers Perrin/Gang & Gang, 2003.

Tucker, Elissa, Tina Kao, Nidhi Verma. *Next-Generation Talent Management: Insights on How Workforce Trends Are Changing the Face of Talent Management.* Hewitt Associates, 2005.

Watson Wyatt Worldwide. *Canadian Organizations Must Work Harder to Productively Engage Employees.* Watson Wyatt's WorkCanada 2004–2005 Survey.

Withers, Pam. "Retention Strategies That Respond to Worker Values." *Workforce Management*, July 2001.

Woodall, Katherine and Charlie Watts. "What 25,000 Employees Globally Say About Communication Effectiveness." *Communication World Bulletin*, January 2005.

Books

Adams, Marilee G. *Change Your Questions, Change Your Life: 7 Powerful Rules for Life and Work.* San Francisco: Berrett-Koehler, 2004.

Bachrach, Bill and Karen Risch (eds.) *Values-Based Selling: The Art of Building High-Trust Client Relationships.* Bachrach & Associates, 1996.

Baker, Dan. *What Happy People Know: How the New Science of Happiness Can Change Your Life for the Better.* New York: St. Martin's Griffin, 2003.

Bohm, David. *On Dialogue.* London and New York: Routledge, 1996.

Bridges, William. *The Way of Transition: Embracing Life's Most Difficult Moments.* Cambridge: Perseus, 2001.

Buckingham, Marcus and Curt Coffman. *First, Break All the Rules: What the World's Greatest Managers Do Differently.* New York: Simon & Schuster, 1999.

Campbell, Ross. *How to Really Love Your Child.* Wheaton: Victor Books, 1977.

Cialdini, Robert. *Influence: The Psychology of Persuasion.* New York: Quill, 1994.

Clarke, Boyd and Ron Crossland. *The Leader's Voice: How Your Communication Can Inspire Action and Get Results!* SelectBooks, 2002.

Clemmer, Jim. *The Leader's Digest: Timeless Principles for Team and Organization Success*. Canada: TCG Press, 2003.

Collins, Jim and Jerry I. Porras. *Built to Last: Successful Habits of Visionary Companies*. New York: HarperBusiness, 1997.

Collins, Jim. *Good to Great: Why Some Companies Make the Leap ... And Others Don't*. New York: HarperCollins, 2001.

Covey, Stephen R. *The Seven Habits of Highly Effective People: Powerful Lessons in Personal Change*. New York: Simon & Schuster, 1989.

Crabb, Larry. *Connecting*. Nashville: Word, 1997.

Csikszentmihalyi, Mihaly. *Flow: The Psychology of Optimal Experience*. New York: HarperPerennial, 1990.

Curran, Charles A. *Understanding: A Necessary Ingredient in Human Belonging*. Chicago: Apple River Press, 1978.

Denning, Stephen. *The Springboard: How Storytelling Ignites Action in Knowledge-Era Organizations*. Butterworth-Heinemann, 2000.

Faber, Adele and Elaine Mazlish. *How to Talk So Kids Will Listen and Listen So Kids Will Talk*. New York: Avon Books, 1980.

Fisher, Roger, William Ury, and Bruce Patton. *Getting to Yes: Negotiating Agreement Without Giving In*. New York: Penguin, 1991.

Frost, Peter J. *Toxic Emotions at Work: How Compassionate Managers Handle Pain and Conflict*. Boston: Harvard Business School Press, 2003.

Fuchs, Nancy. *Our Share of Night, Our Share of Morning: Parenting as a Spiritual Journey*. HarperSanFrancisco, 1996.

Gallwey, W. Timothy. *The Inner Game of Work: Focus, Learning, Pleasure, and Mobility in the Workplace*. New York: Random House, 2000.

Garfield, Charles. *Peak Performers: The New Heroes of American Business*. New York: Avon Books, 1987.

Gladwell, Malcolm. *Blink: The Power of Thinking Without Thinking*. New York: Little, Brown, 2005.

Goleman, Daniel. *Working with Emotional Intelligence*. New York: Bantam Books, 1998.

Goleman, Daniel, Richard Boyatzis, Annie McKee. *Primal Leadership: Realizing the Power of Emotional Intelligence*. Boston: Harvard Business School Press, 2002.

Hendricks, Gay and Kathleen Hendricks. *Conscious Loving: The Journey to Co-Commitment*. New York: Bantam, 1990.

Isaacs, William. *Dialogue and the Art of Thinking Together: A Pioneering Approach to Communicating in Business and in Life*. New York: Doubleday, 1999.

Johnson, Kerry L. *Sales Magic*. Simon & Schuster audio book, 1997.

Kahane, Adam. *Solving Tough Problems: An Open Way of Talking, Listening and Creating New Realities*. San Francisco: Berrett-Koehler, 2004.

Katzenbach, Jon R. and Douglas K. Smith. *The Wisdom of Teams: Creating the High-Performance Organization*. New York: McKinsey & Company, 2003.

Kaye, Beverly and Sharon Jordan-Evans. *Love 'Em or Lose 'Em: Getting Good People to Stay*. San Fransisco: Berrett-Koehler, 2005.

Kotter, John P. and Dan S. Cohen. *The Heart of Change: Real Life Stories of How People Change Their Organizations*. Boston: Harvard Business School Press, 2002.

Loehr, Jim and Tony Schwartz. *The Power of Full Engagement: Managing Energy, Not Time, Is the Key to High Performance and Personal Renewal*. New York: Free Press, 2003.

McManus, Erwin Raphael. *An Unstoppable Force: Daring to Become the Church God Had in Mind*. Loveland: Group Publishing, 2001.

Malandro, Loretta. *Say It Right the First Time: The Power of 100% Accountability*. New York: McGraw-Hill, 2003.

Martin, Roger. *The Responsibility Virus: How Control Freaks, Shrinking Violets – and the Rest of Us – Can Harness the Power of True Partnership*. New York: Basic Books, 2002.

Michalko, Michael. *Thinkertoys: A Handbook of Business Creativity*. Berkeley: Ten Speed Press, 1991.

Parrott, Les and Leslie Parrott, *Saving Your Marriage Before It Starts*. Grand Rapids: Zondervan, 1995.

Senge, Peter M., C. Otto Scharmer, Joseph Jaworski, Betty Sue Flowers. *Presence: An Exploration of Profound Change in People, Organizations, and Society*. New York: Doubleday, 2004.

Senge, Peter M. *The Fifth Discipline: The Art and Practice of the Learning Organization*. New York: Doubleday, 1990.

Senge, Peter M., Art Kleiner (editor), Charlotte Roberts, Richard Ross, George Roth, Bryan Smith. *The Dance of Change: The Challenges to Sustaining Momentum in Learning Organizations*. New York: Doubleday, 1999.

Senge, Peter M., Art Kleiner, Charlotte Roberts, Richard Ross, Bryan Smith. *The Fifth Discipline Fieldbook: Strategies and Tools for Building a Learning Organization*. New York: Doubleday, 1994.

Shaw, Edward. *The Six Pillars of Reality-Based Training: A Practical Guide to Designing and Delivering Training That Works*. Minneapolis: Lakewood, 1997.

Smalley, Gary and John Trent. *The Language of Love: How to Quickly Communicate Your Feelings and Needs*. Pomona: Focus on the Family Publishing, 1988.

Stone, Douglas, Bruce Patton, Sheila Heen. *Difficult Conversations: How to Discuss What Matters Most*. New York: Viking, 1999.

Tournier, Paul. *To Understand Each Other*. Westminster: John Knox Press, 2000.

Ueland, Brenda. *Strength to Your Sword Arm: Selected Writings*. Minnesota: Holy Cow! Press, 1993.

Vella, Jane. *Learning to Listen, Learning to Teach: The Power of Dialogue in Educating Adults*. San Francisco: Jossey-Bass, 1994.

Wheatley, Margaret J. *Leadership and the New Science: Learning About Organization from an Orderly Universe*. San Francisco: Berrett-Koehler, 1999.

Wheatley, Margaret J. *Turning to One Another: Simple Conversations to Restore Hope to the Future*. San Francisco: Berrett-Koehler, 2002.

Index

RELEASE YOUR COMPANY'S
Intelligent Energy
THROUGH POWERFUL CONVERSATIONS
BRADY G. WILSON

- Use this book as a professional personal-development tool throughout your organization. Take advantage of substantial discounts when you purchase multiple copies. Visit our website at www.juiceinc.ca or call us at 519-822-5479 for more details.

- Visit the Juice Resource Centre at www.juiceinc.ca for information about upcoming workshops and speaking engagements, articles and excerpts, and additional Juice resources, including The Juice Check™ – a tool designed to help you measure how much "Intelligent Energy" is released in your work environment.

- Brady Wilson has delivered customized keynote presentations, workshops, seminars, and retreats to hundreds of organizations and thousands of executives internationally. Consider Brady if you're looking for sustainable breakthroughs at your next conference or leadership retreat.

For more information about Brady Wilson or Juice Inc.:
phone: 519-822-5479   email: info@juiceinc.ca
website: www.juiceinc.ca